Redefining Masculinity ©

By

Dean E. Williams Jr. ©

Dedication

This book is dedicated to Irmatrude Grant. She has been the single most influential person in my life. She has been a great mentor and an even greater grandmother. My journey with masculinity started with her and continues even after her passing.

Acknowledgments

This book would not have been written without the following:

- The Burning Man Organization

- Leif and Carol

- Mr. F

- Dr. Nsenga Magnus Farrell

- Dr. Warren Farrell

- Richard V. Reeves

- Cristina Hoff Sommers

- Norah Vincent

- The Crown Inn in Brooklyn (Franklin Ave)

- Mom and Andredale

- Aurora Williams

- Jennifer Broadbent

All of the communities that have helped me become a better person by helping me continue to develop my empathy, understanding, tolerance, and love of humanity. Always working towards being better, always forward.

This work draws on a wide range of historical, philosophical, and contemporary sources. While every effort has been made to credit direct quotations and key intellectual influences, any omissions are unintentional and will be corrected in future editions.

About the Author

Dean Williams is a lifelong learner, scientific skeptic, and generalist whose work sits at the intersection of technology, systems, and human experience. He studied Electrical Engineering and Japanese at the State University of New York at Buffalo, later earning an MBA and a Project Management Professional (PMP) certification. For over twenty years, he has worked as a construction manager, operating inside complex, high-stakes systems that demand coordination, accountability, leadership, and a clear understanding of human behavior under pressure.

Dean's path has included living in Japan through the JET Program as an English teacher and working in multidisciplinary construction environments where leadership styles, cultural norms, and expressions of masculinity vary widely. These experiences shaped his systems-oriented approach and grounded his thinking in how people actually behave when incentives, stress, and identity intersect.

Following the birth of his daughter, Aurora, and the death of his grandmother, Dean turned his attention toward deeper questions of community, grief, responsibility, and meaning. During this period, he became active in the Rotary Club of Harlem and Toastmasters, engaging in service, dialogue, and leadership development. His studies expanded beyond technical disciplines into the humanities, with a focus on empathy, conflict resolution, emotional intelligence, and moral accountability.

Dean's exploration of community and human behavior was further shaped by his experiences at Burning Man, where the culture of radical inclusion, shared responsibility, and communal effort challenged many conventional assumptions about identity, status, and belonging. Through training and service as a Black Rock Ranger, Dean developed practical skills in de-escalation, mediation, situational awareness, and compassionate intervention. Serving in this role required engaging with people from all walks of life in moments of vulnerability, conflict, and celebration, deepening his understanding of human needs, boundaries, and resilience.

As a lifelong learner, Dean has developed technologies, written poetry, essays, opinion pieces, and short fiction, and co-hosted a podcast examining masculinity and society through lived experience rather than ideology. Drawing on his professional background, community work, and personal reflection, he began articulating a perspective rooted not in academic credentialism, but in synthesis, connecting engineering thinking, human systems, and ethical responsibility.

Redefining Masculinity reflects that approach. It is not written from the position of detached authority, but from the belief that meaningful insight does not belong exclusively to institutions. Progress often emerges from individuals willing to observe carefully, think critically, and speak honestly about what they see.

Dean is currently developing a broader framework titled *Tandem Evolution*, which explores how humanity can evolve alongside artificial intelligence without surrendering agency, empathy, or moral grounding. His work is guided by the conviction that thoughtful, responsible voices, especially those shaped by service, systems thinking, and lived experience, are essential to navigating the future.

Foreword

I am the worst in man and the best in man. I have been broken, beaten, and scarred.

I've rolled the dice and lived to tell the story.

I've known pain that left me hollow. Raped, tortured, harassed, and haunted by the weight of suicide.

Yet, I am still here. A man of contradictions: hope and faith, shame and narcissism.

I have objectified and sinned, grasped for control, and manipulated for gain. I've worn vengeance like armor, twisted by fears I refused to name.

I have been the shadow in the corner of your eye; the chill, the ghost, the unspoken.

And yet, I am also light. I am the soul searching for love.

I've learned to hide behind pain. I listen deeply because I know what aching feels like. I comfort others because I've lived where they are.

My empathy is my compass. My daughter, my anchor. My faith, the true North.

To avoid becoming the man my father was, I've spent a lifetime fighting ghosts.

I am pain. I am hope. I am a man holding both truth and noose.

We can reclaim our stories! Not to erase rejection or pain, but to write a new day.

This book is the result of more than 43 years of living, wrestling, and questioning.

It is personal. It is historical. It is human.

As the author, I ask that you read this with an open heart and a skeptical mind. Don't just accept my words, challenge them.

We all carry biases, conscious and unconscious. I had to confront mine to write this.

There are truths in these pages; painful ones, helpful ones, and hidden ones. Some may make you pause. Let them. That's where growth begins.

We try to make life simpler by contrasting dichotomies: red or blue, right or wrong, male or female, strong or weak. But what if it isn't?

What if masculinity isn't fixed, but ever-evolving?

As you read, I invite you to pause. Check in with yourself. Question what you're reading.

Don't just agree - Engage. Doubt. Reflect. Feel.

Look past the debates. Ask yourself what it means to be human, to love, to harm, to heal. Ask who taught you how to be a man. Are you living in your or their definition? Question why you believe what a man should and should not be.

The brain can change. We can change. But only when we make space for new ideas to challenge old ones.

Love can harden us, but it can also break us open. Let this book be an invitation to both.

As a side note, I recognize the evolving science of gender and the deep complexities of identity.

This book welcomes all readers, regardless of your gender or your story. If any language in this book feels biased, know that it is not intentional.

I stand as an ally of humanity.

And I hope this book becomes a spark for the healing conversations we need now more than ever.

Contents

Introduction

The idea for this book began with a series of honest, unfiltered conversations I had with my friend, Mr. F, about dating and relationships.

Mr. F is a no-nonsense, funny, and charismatic man. He's also generally open to new ideas. These qualities have made our dialogues especially rich. These talks sparked the idea for our podcast, *"Black Men: Unmuted, Unplugged, and unapologetic."* A space where we could speak freely about the challenges, contradictions, and growth that comes with being Black men while navigating modern relationships.

During the early brainstorming sessions, we mapped out a few topics we wanted to explore.

Season 1, Episode 1: "Do You Listen to Understand, or Do You Listen to Reply?"

The heart of this episode came from a simple but revealing question: In conversations with a partner or even a potential one. Are you really listening? Do you hear their intentions, feelings, and the truth behind their words? Or do you catch yourself waiting for them to pause so you can jump in with your own thoughts?

I've been guilty of this. And I had to unlearn the habit. My first step toward becoming a better listener was reading Dale Carnegie's *"How to Win Friends and Influence People"*. It gave me the tools to become a better listener, while real-world experience reinforced what I had learned.

Season 1, Episode 2: "Acute vs. Obtuse"

We posed a provocative question: When you ask a woman, "What are you looking for in a man?" you often receive a well-considered list of qualities. However, when you ask, "What do you bring to the table?" the responses tend to range from playful confidence, such as "Me," to discomfort or resistance toward the question itself.

We pushed the conversation even deeper by asking: "Do women seek equality, or do they seek equity? Are some answers vague on purpose, hoping the right man will decode their real desires?"

Our honest assessment brought us to the realization, "Does anyone really have time for that?" The performance of dating, the coded language, and the unspoken expectations can all feel like a game when even the participants do not fully understand.

Who will be the standard bearers? (Season 1 Episode 6)

This was the first conversation that was directly connected to the core of this book.

We had discussed examples of "women behaving badly" in an earlier episode, but I wanted to go deeper to explore responsibility. Specifically: Who holds the line when either a man or a woman crosses it?

If a man behaves in a misogynistic way, who should step in? Should it fall on the woman to correct him? Or is it another man's responsibility to hold him accountable?

Imagine a man catcalling a woman on the street. Should she have to defend herself? Or should a bystanding man call out the behavior?

But here's the complexity: if a man intervenes on her behalf, does he unintentionally take away her agency in that moment?

These questions may not have simple answers, but they matter. We will return to these questions later in this book when we explore power, protection, and humanity.

What I began to realize in these conversations was sobering: The divide between men and women is far greater than I had believed. Both sides are trying to speak, both are trying to listen, but we're often not tuned to the same frequency. As I performed my research for the podcast, the picture became clearer and more troubling. I dove into the world of incels, the growing trend of men falling out of society, the rise of influencers like Andrew Tate, Jordan Peterson, Kevin Samuels, and a disturbing uptick in neo-Nazi rhetoric in the US and Germany. I encountered online cults of misogyny and ideologies feeding masculine resentment.

At the same time, mainstream news reported troubling trends among men: fewer close friendships, higher unemployment, declining purchasing power, and lower scores on the happiness index. Meanwhile, many women were reporting that men seemed more aggressive, more entitled, more dismissive, and some even more dangerous. These conversations weren't just about relationships anymore.

They were about Culture. Power. Fear. Identity.

Some men expressed resentment toward movements like #MeToo and women's rights, seeing them not as corrections to an imbalance, but as threats to a "natural order" between men and women. There are books defending this "decline of men," others urging men to grow and heal, and still others warn about the long-term impact of neglecting boys.

This book is not a comprehensive solution. It is a starting point.

My goal is to spark honest, fact-based, and emotionally grounded dialogue about masculinity; where it stands today, and what happens if we ignore it.

We're reaching a breaking point. And men must take responsibility for both their personal growth and their cultural footprint. But here's the deeper question:

Who holds men accountable?

The answer - The standard bearer.

Every man is a standard bearer for masculinity, whether he knows it or not. We are each responsible for reinforcing, challenging, or reshaping the norms we live by. If we want to redefine masculinity, it has to start with us. It begins with asking:

What is masculinity?

Only when we understand this can we begin the work of moving toward something more whole and something more human. This next statement is not hyperbolic: The future of humanity depends on how we engage this conversation. We're facing immense global challenges such as climate change, artificial intelligence, geopolitical conflict, and mass extinctions. We cannot face the external threats until we can fix the internal societal threats.

And yet, emotionally and spiritually, we are underprepared.

To meet the future head-on, we need a new mindset. One that values collaboration, reflection, and growth over control and fear. History has shown us what happens when power feels threatened: oppression, conflict, destruction. History has also shown us our capacity for reinvention, resilience, and compassion. We're at a crossroads where the needs of the few threaten to eclipse the needs of the many.

The sparks are already flying. So the question becomes: What will we do before the fire engulfs us?

If you're reading this book, you've already taken the first step toward something greater.

Our journey begins with a foundational skill: critical thinking. Before we can redefine masculinity, we must understand how we form beliefs, how we challenge them, and how to open ourselves to change.

The next step takes us into the wonder of biology. We'll explore how genetics shape our development from the womb through adolescence and into adulthood, and how these processes unfold differently across sexes.

From there, we'll zoom out to examine history. How have societies shaped the roles of men and women across time? What have we inherited from ancient ancestors, from Mitochondrial Eve to Lucy, and from Homo sapiens' interactions with Neanderthals and Denisovans?

We'll examine the rise of patriarchy, the fight for gender equality, and the ongoing debates around the Equal Rights Amendment.

Then, we begin to narrow the lens.

We'll explore two core concepts that will guide us throughout this book: Immature Masculinity and Mature Masculinity. I'll introduce these ideas here briefly, and will then expand on them more deeply in later chapters.

- **Immature Masculinity**: blaming others for personal setbacks, dominating in relationships, or seeking power through pain. Minimizing the other. Actions without thought or empathy. Reactionary.

- **Mature Masculinity**, where empathy, consent, communication, service, health, and self-worth lead the way. Thoughtful of others, individual actions and their impact on others.

We'll also study how masculinity has shifted over time through the lens of the Overton Window and how societies have defined, confined, and celebrated different versions of manhood.

From there, we'll begin a process of deconstructing outdated ideals and reconstructing a new vision.

I'll draw heavily from Dr. Warren Farrell's *"The Boy Crisis,"* [1] especially his work on the "purpose void" that many boys and men face today. We'll examine how to navigate this void. How to fill it with meaning instead of resentment.

We'll look at how men can redefine themselves. From being seen as "human doings" to human beings, a term Rick Warren [2] once used that deeply resonated with me. In the final chapters, we'll explore what accountability looks like in action. We'll ask how men can hold themselves and each other to higher standards. *Not perfection, but growth.*

Honesty. Compassion. Integrity. All achieved through Forgiveness, Empathy, Accountability, and Redemption (F.E.A.R.)

Ultimately, this is a book about possibilities. The possibility that men can rewrite not only the script of masculinity, but also the expectations they have for themselves. Those new expectations can ripple outward, strengthening romantic partnerships, friendships, families, and communities.

After the wave of mass shootings that followed COVID lockdowns, the media began focusing more on the growing crisis facing men and boys. Some social critics argued that in uplifting women and girls, society had unintentionally left boys behind. Others believed this decline was a byproduct or even an intention of modern feminism. Regardless of perspective, what became clear was that many young men were lost, and they were finding dangerous comfort in toxic ideologies.

I focused much of my research on three books that offered critical insight into this subject:

- The Boy Crisis: Why Our Boys Are Struggling and What We Can Do about It by Warren Farrell, Ph.D., and John Gray, Ph.D. [3]

- The War Against Boys: How Misguided Policies Are Harming Our Young Men by Christina Hoff Sommers [4]

- Of Boys and Men: Why the Modern Male Is Struggling, Why It Matters, and What to Do About It by Richard V. Reeves [5]

These works helped me flesh out the ideas that formed the backbone of this project. I'll reference other sources along the way to deepen and clarify key points. But here's something important: this book is not a lecture. It's a conversation.

You, the reader, have a role in it.

I encourage you to challenge what you're reading. Look for supporting or contradictory evidence. Think critically, but also empathetically. Let other voices and ideas join this journey. Be open, even if it's uncomfortable, especially if it's uncomfortable.

This may be your first time stepping into this kind of reflection. Embrace it. That's where change begins. Welcome to the first steps in becoming a better man and, more importantly, a better human. To the women reading this book or to those who notice a man reading it, I ask for your support. Support the men who are trying, sincerely, to change not just for ourselves, but in how society sees us and how we see each other.

I recognize something many of you already know too well: that a man's physical presence. His masculinity, his build, and his skin tone can shift the energy in a room. As a Black man, I know that shift intimately. I've seen how my presence alone can alter someone's posture, tighten their voice, or raise their guard. I also understand the fear of being harassed or worse, for simply walking, driving, or existing while Black. These experiences have shaped my understanding of consent, empathy, and the urgent need for men and women to work together toward equity, not dominance.

This book will not shy away from these themes. We'll explore them with honesty, humility, and with the hope that they lead to real conversations and real change. To the women who care about the men in your lives, including your brothers, partners, sons, students, or friends, your voice matters too.

I invite you to be part of this dialogue. Tell us how we can do better. Help us build the bridge. And when the time comes, I hope you'll feel safe enough to reflect on what it means to be female standard bearers in this evolving conversation.

On a personal note…

Years ago, I found myself asking:

— How do I get what I want from people?

— How do I influence them without giving up who I am?

I had seen others succeed through manipulation or dominance, often disregarding the humanity of the person in front of them.

I was tired of being the "nice guy" who got overlooked. That's when I decided to read a book that kept showing up in conversations: "How to Win Friends and Influence People" by Dale Carnegie.[6]

I remember holding it in my hands and saying, "Book, you and I are going to go far." And I wasn't wrong. What I didn't expect was this: the secret to influence wasn't control, it was empathy. To truly connect with others, I had to start caring about them. I had to want what was best for them. At first, I was mad about it. It felt unfair; the cheat code was to do more work. I took a moment to reflect on what I wanted in life, and I started applying the principles from the book. I opened my heart, listened more, showed up differently, and the world responded. My heart grew ten sizes that day, and the people of Whoville rejoiced.

As we move forward together, I'll share more of these personal stories; real moments that shaped how I think about masculinity, maturity, and growth. I want to offer you a full picture, not of perfection, but of continued practice and improvement.

This isn't about having all the answers. It's about becoming the kind of man who's willing to challenge oneself to be better.

Chapter 1
Critical Thinking

As you read this book, I invite you to engage with the content critically. This requires more than passive reading; it requires active participation in the process of thinking. Just as we must be active in our own personal growth, so too must we be active in the way we consume information. No one is a better advocate for you than you are. You care most about your well-being, so it is in your best interest to ensure that the information you are taking in is logical, unbiased, and grounded in truth.

If you're familiar with critical thinking strategies or scientific skepticism, think of this section as a refresher, a chance to sharpen your skills. Critical thinking is not just about finding flaws in others' arguments but about refining your own thinking to make more informed, thoughtful decisions. This book is designed to provoke, to challenge your assumptions, and to encourage you to think deeply. We all have biases, and part of critical thinking is learning to identify and understand those biases, especially the ones we may not even be aware of.

Our biases are part of our evolution. They serve us by helping us make quick decisions in situations where we don't have all the information.[7] These "mental shortcuts" are called heuristics. Strategies we use to simplify complex problems. Heuristics allow us to make judgments based on previous knowledge or experience, guiding us through uncertainty. In many ways, these shortcuts help us survive. But when we don't recognize them, they can also lead us astray.

Critical thinking involves recognizing and challenging our biases, staying open-minded, and relying on well-supported, factual information. It requires awareness of logical fallacies and how they can surface in our daily lives. For example, we might all know people who argue from personal belief rather than evidence. This is one of the many forms of faulty reasoning we need to recognize and avoid in our own thinking.

When I am uncertain about the reliability of a source or the political leanings of the media I consume, I turn to resources like *Allsides.com* and the *Ad Fontes Media Bias Chart* to verify the credibility of information. This habit of checking bias is something my daughter and I practice together. Whenever we are curious about a topic, whether it's "Why is the sky blue?" "Why do goats scream like humans?" or "What would happen if you threw a baseball at the speed of light?" We first do a "bias check."

We ask ourselves, "What do we already know? And where might we be biased in our thinking?" Before diving into sources like *Google, ChatGPT, or Wikipedia*, we make sure we are approaching the subject with a fresh, open perspective. This ensures we don't fall into the Dunning-Kruger effect, which is the trap of thinking we know more than we do. We aim to remain humble in our knowledge, assuming we don't have all the answers but are actively searching to fill in the gaps. By starting with simple, clear explanations (like asking "Explain it like I'm five"), we build our understanding in manageable steps.

This method of inquiry and exploration, learned from my grandmother, is how we approach new information as a family. She always told me,

"Knowledge is power, and it's the one thing no one can take away from you." This mindset has shaped how I process new ideas and how I want you, the reader, to approach this book. By fostering a mindset of inquiry, skepticism, and empathy, we can work toward not just understanding ideas but transforming the way we engage with them.

When you read this book, remember to check for biases. Both your own and those that might be embedded in the information you encounter. A bias is any belief that influences the way we interpret the world and make decisions. Our brains develop these biases as survival mechanisms, helping us make decisions quickly when time or information is limited. But biases also push us toward the familiar and comfortable, even when that comfort is based on flawed reasoning. Some of these biases are unconscious, while others are conscious choices we knowingly make when we interpret new information.

By being aware of these biases, we can take active steps to think more critically. We can challenge our assumptions, stay open to new perspectives, and engage with others empathetically. This is how we improve our ability to think critically, not just for the sake of intellectual exercise, but to make better decisions for our lives and the world around us.

In the book "Determined: A Science of Life without Free Will", Robert Sapolsky argues that we are incapable of exercising free will. In an interview with The New York Times, Hope Reese summarizes Sapolsky's position: "Dr. Sapolsky confronts and refutes the biological and philosophical arguments for free will. He contends that we are not free agents, but that biology, hormones, childhood and life circumstances coalesce to produce actions that we merely feel were ours to choose." [8] This view contends with the idea that we are creatures of habit and products of our evolutionary history. Our biases, like our actions, are shaped by our environment and our evolutionary development.

In an episode of the Intelligence Squared podcast titled "Debate: Free Will is an Illusion," the dichotomy of free will is discussed in depth. The conversation between Susan Blackmore and Kevin Mitchell offers valuable insights into how we should view human actions. If we are products of evolution and our environment, our biases and actions cannot be separated from this broader context, which relates directly to the overall discussion about biases. [9]

Critical thinking requires effort and discipline. There is a belief that part of the divisiveness in the United States stems from a lack of empathy and understanding, and I subscribe to that view. Many societal issues could be resolved by taking the time to challenge information presented to us, seeking to understand the reasoning behind it, and acknowledging the emotions involved. Critical thinking also requires self-awareness, i.e., checking in with your feelings and asking yourself whether you are being receptive to new ideas. If not, it is important to explore why that is. Understanding yourself is the first step toward understanding others.

So how does this all connect to redefining masculinity? In Mature Masculinity, we seek truth to use as a tool to complete ourselves and uplift our communities. Truth can take many forms: the information we use to make daily decisions, the process of self-reflection, and our understanding of who we truly are. It also includes an honest evaluation of our relationships, both in their current state and in terms of where we hope to take them. Truth requires us to confront both our conscious and unconscious biases and do the difficult work of engaging with new and old information.

Questions like:

- How does this new information make me feel?

- How do I process it?

- Are you checking in with yourself to understand how you feel about the information, and

- Asking how it might affect others?

In Immature Masculinity, men accept information that makes them feel good or reinforces their worldview without questioning whether this acceptance is due to bias. This kind of masculinity does not question the source of the information or its intent, or the potential harm it may pose to them or their community.

In contrast, Mature Masculinity prompts questions such as: Who is relaying the information? What is the information? Is it an opinion or a fact? Where did they obtain the information? Why are they sharing it? Why now? How was it received, and how is it being presented? When was it introduced into the discourse, and is it still relevant today? These are valid and important questions to ask in order to critically engage with information. These questions are critical to adopting critical thinking strategies.

Being able to fact-check and critically evaluate information is essential. This includes developing the skills to read and comprehend research papers, cross-referencing multiple reliable sources, and verifying the credibility of primary sources. Consulting trusted fact-checking organizations, such as FactCheck.org, Snopes.com, or Media Bias/Fact Check, can offer additional validation and perspective.

When relying on research, it is especially important to prioritize meta-analyses over single studies. Meta-analyses combine the results of multiple studies and conduct statistical analyses to provide more reliable conclusions, offering a broader perspective than individual research papers.

One of my favorite tools in critical thinking is understanding logical fallacies. Logical fallacies are errors in reasoning that can undermine the validity and soundness of an argument. They often involve flawed logic, misleading language, or faulty assumptions. Recognizing and understanding logical fallacies is important for critical thinking because they can deceive or manipulate the audience and weaken the strength of an argument.

Some examples of logical fallacies include:

Slippery Slope: This fallacy involves the belief that one action will inevitably lead to more extreme consequences.

Example:

A common argument against gun regulation is the belief that banning certain guns will eventually lead to a ban on all guns. This argument assumes that any restriction will result in total prohibition, despite no evidence supporting such a claim. In reality, gun regulations already exist, such as bans on fully automatic weapons and background checks, without eliminating gun ownership. Furthermore, a complete ban would require a constitutional amendment, which would need approval from two-thirds of Congress and three-fourths of the US states. At least 12 states would never support such a change, making it nearly impossible to repeal the Second Amendment. Constitutional rights have faced reasonable restrictions in the past without being abolished, such as limits on free speech and religious practices. Regulation does not equate to elimination, and the fear that all guns will be banned overlooks both legal and political realities.

Straw Man Argument: This fallacy occurs when someone misrepresents another person's argument to make it easier to attack or refute.

Example:

Suppose your friend argues that global warming is causing harm due to rising sea levels, which will affect coastlines. In that case, you might respond by saying, "So you're saying we should completely shut down all industries and live without electricity just to stop the sea levels from rising? That's unrealistic and would destroy the economy." This response distorts the original argument by exaggerating it, making it easier to dismiss. The original point was about addressing rising sea levels, not shutting down entire industries.

Appeal to Emotion: This fallacy manipulates emotions such as fear, pity, or sympathy to persuade someone, bypassing logical reasoning or evidence.

Example:

An argument might be made that we need to change gun laws to keep guns out of the hands of minorities because of the danger they pose to society. This is not only misleading but also contrary to evidence, which shows that white men commit the majority of mass shootings. A majority of gun violence is perpetrated inside a community and rarely reaches outside of that community.[10]

I also recommend reviewing the Wikipedia page on different types of logical fallacies as a starting point. Try to think of examples from your own experiences or arguments you've heard, and you'll be surprised at how often logical fallacies appear on both sides of an issue. Recognizing logical fallacies takes practice, but with time, you will develop a sharper ability to spot them. Another useful resource is the podcast The Skeptics' Guide to the Universe, which regularly reviews logical fallacies.

Critical Thinking and Scientific Research

While writing this book, I made a conscious effort to be an active and critical reader during my research. In reading *The Boy Crisis*, I came across a discussion about circumcision and its hypothesized connection to Alexithymia, a condition that makes it difficult not just to express feelings but to identify them in the first place. Dr. Farrell references preliminary research on three hundred men, suggesting that they may have a 20 percent greater chance than intact boys of experiencing Alexithymia.

This piqued my curiosity, so I decided to look for more recent studies or meta-analyses on the phenomenon. I found a meta-analysis titled

"Critical Evaluation of Contrasting Evidence on Whether Male Circumcision Has Adverse Psychological Effects: A Systematic Review", which included 11,173 males. The conclusion of the study reads: "The highest quality evidence suggests that neonatal and later circumcision has limited or no short-term or long-term adverse psychological effects." [11]

To Dr. Farrell's credit, he did mention that the study he referenced was preliminary, which prompted me to do further research.[12] This is a critical example of how some authors do not take this additional step of verification.

If you find this as fascinating as I do (adjusts glasses and pocket protector), continue reading about these subjects. Understanding how our brains have evolved to survive is paramount to understanding why critical thinking is important. We evolved to believe in things we interacted with through our senses, a process that has evolved over millions of years. Homo sapiens have been around for about 300,000 years, and misinformation has been a challenge since language first emerged around 150,000 years ago. For further reading, I would recommend *The Evolution of Cognitive Bias* by Martie G. Haselton, Daniel Nettle, and Damian R. Murray[13] and *Behave* by Dr. Roberty Sapolsky.

Reading scientific research papers can be a daunting task, but the age of AI offers an opportunity to bridge the gap between scientists and the public. The continued need for in-depth scientific research is essential. Scientific research provides the foundation for AI models. The better the public understands the scientific method and research publication literacy, the more it will encourage scientists to improve their work before publishing. We will expect more from journals and studies. Meta-analyses and Bayesian analysis will serve as the litmus tests for what information gets incorporated into AI models. This information can be reliably used to influence public policy and societal progress.

So, how does this shape the conversation? Throughout the following chapters, we'll explore evidence-based facts that you may have been told to ignore or that you may not believe to be true. I will present the current scientific understanding, as of 2025, and associated data to support these discussions. As critical thinkers, it's essential to review data and sources, checking and double-checking against the latest research and updated studies. Wherever possible, I will rely on meta-analysis studies as the foundation for any concepts or ideas presented.

Let's continue with a brief review of the scientific method and how it relates to meta-analysis and Bayesian analysis. The scientific method is a systematic approach used to acquire knowledge about the natural world through empirical evidence and logical reasoning. The key steps in the scientific method include observation, hypothesis formation, experimentation, data collection, analysis, and conclusion. The brilliance of the scientific community lies in the peer review process, where studies must meet rigorous standards before being published. The more prestigious the journal, the more stringent these requirements are.

The scientific community also self-regulates. If a study is found to be misleading or contains misinformation, it is retracted. When reviewing a research paper, tools such as the *P-value* which indicates whether or not the initial hypothesis has significance or if there is another factor at play; or Bayesian Analysis, are used by researchers to assess the quality of the study. Bayesian Analysis is considered a better indicator because it relies on results from previous studies, whereas the P-value is based solely on information within the study. There are instances where a hypothesis is adjusted to align with the results, which results in a higher P-value. This practice is called P-hacking and is strongly discouraged and erroneous. The pressures of publishing and the rise of fake research papers have led to an increase in P-hacking. Geoff Cummings offers an insightful YouTube video titled "The Dance of the P- Value."

***	.001	Very highly significant!!!	There IS an effect. Definitely, for sure!	Elation!! Exuberance!! Smugness?	Nobel Prize, Tenure, Research grant
**	.01	Highly significant!!	There is an effect.	Great pleasure, Dancing, Drinking	PhD, Prize, Top publication
*	.05	Significant (phew!)	Most likely, there is an effect.	Relief, Cheerfulness	Consolation prize, Fair publication
?	.10	Approaching significance	Almost. Probably an effect, but low power?	Frustration, 'if only'	Counselling, stress leave
p>.10		Nonsignificant	No effect (effect is zero?)	Despair, depression	Medication, Reconsider life goals

Intro Statistics 9: The Dance of the P-value[14]

Scientific Research and the Role of Statistics

As with any system, there are bugs. Scientific study requires continual improvement in both the quality of research and the accessibility of information to the public. Academia is increasingly focused on regulating the rise of fake research papers and ending the incentivizing of publishing papers with high confidence rates. Resources like Google Scholar, JSTOR, and the Library of Congress are excellent starting points for navigating scientific papers. Websites like Retraction Watch also help track papers that have been retracted for various reasons, contributing to the checks and balances that form the foundation of scientific research.

If you want a deeper dive into understanding how to read scientific papers, I recommend seeking out books on this subject. Please remember that unless you have been trained as a scientist or an academic, it takes years of study to fully understand how to interpret and analyze scientific research. This is why the consensus of the scientific community is so crucial. Scientists are the experts in the scientific process, and they have their pulse on the current, evidence-based, peer-reviewed science. In many ways, scientists today are the modern-day librarians of Alexandria.

Statistics: Unveiling the Numbers

One last area of study to touch on is statistics. We briefly discussed P-values earlier, but it's important to delve deeper into the role of statistics in scientific research. The beauty of statistics lies in its ability to distill complex data into meaningful insights. By incorporating multiple layers of data, statistics can reveal both correlations and causations within a single graph. However, statistics can also be manipulated to mislead or misrepresent the story that the data is telling. It is crucial to understand not just the information presented but also how the data is represented, as well as how it can be misrepresented.

To help illustrate this, let's consider a set of questions that encourage deeper understanding of data and statistics:

"What is statistical analysis? What are the best ways to interpret data or a graph? What should we look for to ensure that we, as readers, are not misinterpreting the data, and that the author is not misrepresenting it?"

Statistical analysis involves collecting, organizing, analyzing, interpreting, and presenting data to uncover patterns, relationships, and insights that lead to meaningful conclusions. It includes a range of techniques, such as descriptive statistics, hypothesis testing, regression analysis, and data visualization.

Many of the same critical thinking steps that we use to verify claims or statements also apply when reading statistics. The key is confirming the reliability of the information and referencing alternate sources when reviewing the same data. Additionally, skills like numeracy (the ability to understand and use numbers) and literacy (the ability to read and understand data) play a significant role in how we interpret statistics. Our biases can impair our ability to interpret data accurately, making self-awareness an essential part of critical evaluation.

In the study titled "Motivated Numeracy and Enlightened Self-Government", the authors explore how bias affects our interpretation of empirical data. They write, "In our experiment, we presented subjects with a difficult problem that required them to draw valid causal inferences from empirical data. As expected, subjects highest numeracy, those with a strong ability to use quantitative information, did significantly better than those with lower numeracy when the data was presented as results from a study on a new skin rash treatment. However, when the same data was presented in the context of a study on a gun control ban, subjects' responses became politically polarized and even less accurate. Interestingly, this polarization did not decrease among subjects highest numeracy; instead, it increased."[15]

This outcome supported ICT (Intelligent-Causal Thinking), which predicted that more numerate subjects would use their quantitative reasoning abilities selectively, shaping their interpretation of data to align with results that best match their political beliefs. We must always be aware of our biases and their potential to color the way we decode information. The beauty of the human brain is its ability to change and adapt. Our brains possess a remarkable ability known as neuroplasticity.

Critical Thinking and Neuroplasticity

Neuroscientist Tara Swift writes, "Neuroplasticity is the brain's ability to change itself constantly by creating new neural pathways and losing those which are no longer used. Encouraging the brain's neuroplasticity is the key to sustained adult learning and emotional intelligence, which will help the brain remain open-minded, intuitive and able to overcome biases throughout adulthood."[16]

A recent study sheds light on a potential path to conquering our biases and exercising neuroplasticity. The study involved 1,642 Americans during the 2020 election count, testing how beliefs about election fraud changed based on hypothetical outcomes. The study found that participants' beliefs in fraud increased when their preferred candidate lost, and decreased when their candidate won. These shifts were more pronounced among those with stronger partisan preferences, illustrating partisan asymmetry: a tendency for biases to shape our perceptions of facts. A Bayesian model of rational belief updating, which considered beliefs in the true winner, fraud prevalence, and the beneficiary of fraud, more accurately accounted for this than alternative models. [17] These findings suggest that changing such beliefs may require addressing multiple key beliefs at once, rather than simply debunking misinformation directly.

Studies like this one are being conducted at universities worldwide. Critical thinking is essential for empowering the public to have greater control over government and to build bridges of understanding and mutual respect. We do not always have to agree on solutions, but we must agree on the facts and be willing to adjust our mindset as those facts evolve.

Critical Thinking in Everyday Life

I realize that this journey through critical thinking may feel daunting. However, there is a point to all of this. If you absorbed any of this information, you may start to notice that conversations or arguments may contain logical fallacies, or you might question whether you are using sound reasoning or being bias yourself. Once you're introduced to critical thinking, it begins to show up everywhere. It's similar to someone pointing out that a friend hisses when they pronounce a word with an 's' in it. Once you hear it, you're surprised to realize it was there all along. Why didn't you notice it before? It's because our brains adapt to our environment, and we only become conscious of things when we deliberately focus on them. Critical thinking works in much the same way.

On a personal note, I had a friend who once gave me a book on critical thinking and logical fallacies. I initially dismissed it, blinded by my ego. I thought I was already a critical thinker and didn't need further input on the subject. I believed I was the smartest person in the room. I remember debating with others and not understanding why they couldn't see things from my point of view. I was convinced that my reasoning was sound and that anyone who listened would eventually come around to my way of thinking.

I talked to my friends about this, and they pointed out that some of my arguments were based on logical fallacies. It took me some time to accept this feedback, but eventually, I started studying logic, both mathematical and reasoning-based logic. I wanted to incorporate logical reasoning into my daily life, which led me to scientific skepticism through *The Skeptics' Guide to the Universe*.[18]

This happened around the same time I began reading *How to Win Friends and Influence People*.[19] Both books are similar in how they approach relationships with people: one from an intellectual standpoint and the other from an emotional intelligence perspective. In reading *How to Win Friends and Influence People*, I learned about emotional intelligence and how it helps build stronger connections and fosters understanding.

I had always believed life was black and white, no gray areas. But as I continued my reading and self-reflection, I came to understand that humans live in the gray areas of life. It is here, in the space between extremes, that intelligence and emotional intelligence must work together.

Chapter Summary

This chapter lays out why critical thinking has to be an active practice, not something we assume we already know how to do. I walk through how our biases, instincts, and even the limits of our supposed free will shape the way we interpret information, and why we have to push back against those forces with evidence, verification, and a willingness to question ourselves. I tie this directly to masculinity, because Immature Masculinity absorbs whatever feels comfortable, while Mature Masculinity slows down, asks harder questions, and demands truth over convenience. Throughout, I show how tools like media bias checks, logical fallacies, and scientific research methods keep us honest and help us grow. At its core, this chapter is about building the discipline to think clearly so we can become better men, better people, and better contributors to our communities.

Main Points

- Critical thinking is an active, disciplined process of evaluating information that demands awareness of biases, logical fallacies, and the quality of evidence (with an emphasis on scientific method, meta-analyses, and statistics).

- Human biases and behavior are shaped by evolution, environment, and possibly constrained free will, yet neuroplasticity and deliberate practice give us the capacity to change how we think.

- Mature Masculinity is defined by applying critical thinking and empathy to how men consume information, question assumptions, and make decisions, in contrast to Immature Masculinity that accepts comforting narratives without scrutiny.

Chapter 2

A Brief History of Masculinity

Plants, Power, War and the men that love them

Now that we have a healthy inoculation against misinformation, fortified with a dose of critical thinking, we can begin our journey. Before we discuss "Redefining Masculinity", it is important to understand how masculinity developed, the history of the patriarchy, traditional roles men and women have played in society, and where we stand today.

I will draw on information grounded in the current, widely accepted scientific consensus. The aim is not to overwhelm, but to give a clear historical foundation for understanding masculinity.

I will purposely avoid discussing the history of sex and gender in this chapter; a later section will address gender roles specifically. This book does not cover the ranges of sexual identity or gender identity, as there are already many authoritative works on those subjects that are considered the gold standards. Some books of note are:

- My Gender Workbook by Kate Bornstein

- The ABC's of LGBT by Ash Hardell

- Stone Butch Blues by Leslie Feinberg

- Trans Bodies, Trans Selves edited by Laura Erickson-Schroth

- Middlesex by Jeffrey Eugenides

- Orlando by Virginia Woolf

As you read, this is an excellent moment to put those newly minted critical thinking skills into practice.

The Past

In archeology, our friend the fossil records show that the first hominids: *Denisovans, Neanderthal,* and their younger, more populous cousins, *Homosapiens,* at some point lived and interacted with other species that existed during their respective periods. At times, they got to know each other well…. biblically speaking. In a 2018 paper, further evidence was discovered that Denisovans and Neanderthals interacted with each other and even mated. "Neanderthals and Denisovans are extinct groups of hominids that separated from each other more than 390,000 years ago.

Here we present the genome of '*Denisova 11*', a bone fragment from Denisova Cave (Russia) and show that it comes from an individual who had a Neanderthal mother and a Denisovan father. The father, whose genome bears traces of Neanderthal ancestry, came from a population related to a later Denisovan found in the cave.

The mother came from a population more closely related to Neanderthals who lived later in Europe, than to an earlier Neanderthal found in Denisova Cave, suggesting that migrations of Neanderthals between eastern and western Eurasia occurred sometime after 120,000 years ago. The finding of a first-generation Neanderthal–Denisovan offspring among the small number of archaic specimens sequenced to date suggests that mixing between Late Pleistocene hominin groups was common when they met."[20] The human genome, once decoded, has shown us that remnants of the Denisovan and Neanderthal ancestors live in us today. Remnants of Neanderthal DNA are mostly found in people with European Ancestry, and Denisovan DNA is mostly found in people with Asian ancestry."

Why is knowing our genetic history important? It is important to understand that part of the reason we were able to survive past our cousins is because of our intellect. Jared Diamond in Guns, Germs, and Steel talks extensively about how human societies transitioned from being nomadic hunter-gatherers to settled agriculturalists, and how this transition was driven by the need for more reliable food sources and the development of new technologies. He argues that human ingenuity and the development of agriculture fundamentally changed human societies, leading to the rise of hierarchical structures, resource control, and large-scale social organization.[21]

Yuval Noah Harari, in *Sapiens: A Brief History of Humankind*, similarly explores how the Cognitive Revolution and the Agricultural Revolution dramatically shifted the trajectory of human development. Harari highlights the creativity and ingenuity of humans in adapting to and transforming their environments, but also emphasizes the costs of these changes—such as the shift away from the egalitarian hunter-gatherer lifestyle to more hierarchical, resource-based societies.[22]

We are social creatures, as are all descendants of the great apes. We see this today in the natural habitats of our closest ancestors. In that social order, each member has a role based on their gender. Females of the species were tasked with child rearing, domestication, and gathering. Males of the species would hunt for food, provide shelter and protection. These roles were not mutually exclusive to the sexes. Some women were also part of the hunting parties, and some men also took care of the children.

Dr. Vivek Venkataraman, in his article "Ancient Men Were Hunters and Women Were Gatherers, Right? Wrong", argues that the evidence shows that there were women who would hunt alongside men, or aid in the development of tools for hunting, or help with trapping the prey:

"There were women who would hunt alongside men or aid in the development of tools for hunting or help with trapping the prey."[23]

The reason women did not take on a more active role in hunting, as elaborated in 1970 by feminist anthropologist Judith Brown, is that the demands of hunting conflict with the provision of child care:

"The reason for women not taking on more of an active role in hunting... is that the demands of hunting conflict with the provision of child care." [24]

In a recent review of women's hunting, which surveyed traditional societies around the world, the authors found that pregnant or lactating women do not often hunt. Furthermore, those with dependents only hunt when child care is available or when rich hunting grounds are close to camp:

"Pregnant or lactating women do not often hunt, and those with dependents only hunt when child care is available or rich hunting grounds are close to camp."[25] One of the first forms of hunting is Persistence hunting. Our species is specifically adept at this form of hunting. We have sweat glands and hair on our heads to protect us from the sun. We have the endurance to track down any animal over a long distance. When it came time to leave an area in search of food, the camp would pick up and leave in search of more fertile land. In every camp, there were men, women, elders, and leaders all working towards the survival of the species. Most of these societies were egalitarian, where all people were equal, deserving of equal rights and opportunities. The current scientific consensus is that men and women were equal in hunter-gatherer societies. So what happened?

Greed!. Wait, it can't be that simple. Based on my research, it is as simple as that. In a study that reviewed the cause of socioeconomic disparity in 89 hunter-gatherer societies along the Pacific Coast of North America, the results were as follows:

"Our results indicate that the most important predictors are related to the spatiotemporal distribution of resources. Specifically, higher reliance on and ownership of clumped aquatic (primarily salmon) versus wild plant resources is associated with greater political-economic inequality, measuring the latter as a composite of internal social ranking, unequal access to food resources, and the presence of slavery. Variables indexing population pressure, scalar stress, and intergroup conflict exhibit little or no correlation with variation in equality. These results are consistent with models positing that hierarchy will emerge when individuals or coalitions (e.g., kin groups) control access to economically defensible, highly clumped resource patches, and use this control to extract benefits from subordinates such as productive labor and political allegiance in a patron-client system."[26]

To summarize this passage, the closer a group of people is, the more likely they are to use their abundance to gain support or labor from others who work for them. This is important because it moves us closer to where the transition occurs from egalitarian to hierarchical systems.

When an argument is made that men were born to be dominant, leaders, rulers, providers and all controlling, remind them that their ancestors believed in equality amongst the group and that everyone had a place at the table. Our society changed from everyone having a chance at eating at the table to some eating at the head of the table and others eating scraps from the table. We understand why scientists believe an egalitarian group would switch to a hierarchical group, but what was the catalyst for the patriarchy? My hypothesis is War!!!!

War, was it as good for you as it was for me?

In Jared Diamond's Guns, Germs, and Steel, the role of war in the context of human history and societal development is discussed, particularly with regard to how war served as a means of transferring wealth and resources. Diamond explores how early societies, particularly those that transitioned from hunter-gatherer to agricultural economies, had to contend with the rise of neighboring groups who sought to gain control over their resources. He suggests that the development of warfare was intimately linked to the need to protect these newfound agricultural surpluses and permanent settlements.[27]

How are men the perfect weapon?

They are the stronger of the human species; men are not saddled by child rearing and lactation, and they have fewer hormonal fluctuations compared to women. Men do require more calories than women, but with agriculture and animal domestication, food supply chains and food stores were built up and could allow for travel anywhere. In a study titled "The Importance of Physical Strength to Human Males," the authors discuss the correlation between strength and physical aggression in males and how men evolved to resolve conflict through aggression. In their conclusion, they note, "The assessment mechanisms in the minds of men and women that track and respond to cues of upper-body strength also testify to the importance fighting ability had for our ancestors. And finally the persistence of association between upper-body strength and psychological and behavioral variables in modern men shows how powerful the selection pressures were; physically stronger men have been shown to feel more entitled to better outcomes, to set a lower threshold for the triggering of anger and physical aggression, to have more self-favoring attitudes about income redistribution, and to believe more in the utility warfare" [28]

As a side note, the study also noted, as a result of their data analysis, a correlation between an actor's perceived ability to fight, how they present on screen and their political affiliation. "Consistent with the hypothesis that physical strength is linked to positive views of the utility of warfare, many of the action stars categorized as left-wing were indeed physically less imposing than their right-wing counterparts. For example, Nicholas Cage, Tom Cruise, Pierce Brosnan, and Keanu Reeves are prominent left-wing action stars but do not appear to have the same physiques as Schwarzenegger, Stallone, or Chuck Norris.[29]

In "Why war is a man's game," the author offers up another advantage that men have: less cost for participation in war. As with the previous study, one male can reproduce with six women and produce six offspring in 10 months. A woman can only produce one child in 10 months. The male population can be replenished more quickly, and help increase a group's military might. Men also compete against other men in a society. Based on this study, the competition is a reason for the male push towards war. One of the more interesting parts of this study is that the use of male combatants provides a greater probability of winning a war. This greater probability is great for the group's resource and reproductive successes. The destruction of a male removes a military and reproductive threat against a warring group. Many cultures understood this. Men took on the greater risk by sacrificing themselves for group gain, and with great sacrifice comes a greater reward. This is a domineering principle in business and life. [30]

From these studies we find that men have the best variables to make effective combatants. Where does that lead us today? We discussed how the change from an egalitarian society, due to agriculture and static resources, led to a hierarchical society. Once power is gained, holding on to power then becomes the next major step. The best way to hold on to power is to ensure that your family's succession plan is the succession of your power. Many societies or groups of people have a familial trait that binds them together. As a group grows, resources diminish. As resources diminish, people will choose to either settle elsewhere or find a new food source. What do you do if there is no other place to settle? You are forced to move and take over the land of others. There were no negotiations. One did what they had to do to survive. To feed the multiple generations in my group, I will need to find resources for them.

Once we go to war with another group, if we win, we can take their resources and bolster our ranks by killing their men and reproducing with their women. Their sons will be our sons and become our tribe.

The initial cause for war was for resources; however, as groups of people started taking on hierarchical roles, those who had an abundance wanted more, and those who did not have wanted to have what those in abundance had. To be successful at war, you need to use the best weapon you have. Men. To get men to follow you, there was the grand promise of honor, abundance of resources, and women. The men who could make these promises and garner support within their societies were made leaders, rulers, even kings…. this is at the rudimentary level.

Now, let's talk more about men and why we are an important tool in war.

What if I told you that our early ancestors would sleep around often? Some researchers believe the male penis's shape evolved to remove semen from other men during copulation.[31] There is also a study that notes that the female orgasm is designed to allow the sperm of her more appealing suitor to travel deeper inside her.[32] This is part of the current evolutionary understanding of how our sex organs evolved. So what stopped the *"key parties?"* Sexually Transmitted Diseases. In the study "Disease dynamics and costly punishment can foster socially imposed monogamy," the authors conclude that due to the rise in agriculture and societies, these societies switched from polygamy to monogamy. They conclude that this occurred with self-imposed punishments for polygamy. STIs can cause sterility and other health comorbidities that are seen as detrimental to society. With the move to monogamy, the pool of eligible bachelors and bachelorettes would become a closed loop.[33]

In war, the winner gets the spoils. In war, any woman taken captive would become a suitable mate. Since monogamy became the way of life, a man would now take on a single wife and a single family. His role would change to protector of his family and of his society. So how does this connect with war? As stated previously, war is a means to gain resources or protect resources. War is the path that the powerful use to remain powerful, all the while planting seeds of potential power in the powerless. Men are offered land, money, fame and women to go to war, all to help bolster and support the leader and expand their rule. Men were slowly changed from members of an egalitarian society to believing that they were owed more due to their physical prowess and power.

We are Men!! We should be feared and can take what we want from the weak (said while thumping one's chest). As societies began to move away from thinking in terms of communal needs, where all could contribute; to individual familial needs, where male contribution was linked to the leader's success, women became second-class citizens in society.

The rise of the second class

In this book, I have set out to show that the switch to agriculture led to war, which led to the creation of masculinity in its current form. Our goal is to redefine a word that no man living had a say in the formation of, but is a product of.

If you've stayed awake to this point, we have discussed how agricultural changes were instrumental to changes in the power dynamic in human social groups. The fall of the egalitarian society and the rise of the patriarchy and the second-class citizenry of women. The secondary role of women can be seen as far back as Egyptian and Judeo religious texts; even in the epics of Gilgamesh and Beowulf, our earliest pieces of literature. In the local clusters, power was held by successful familial lines; lines that had the military and resources to govern a people. What were the roles of women and men in some of these early hierarchical societies? Women were mainly responsible for child rearing and domestication. They played larger roles in agriculture and production when men went off to war. This is the reason why a male child was more favored than a female. A male child could take on many of the tasks of their fathers, as their fathers went to war. How do you push boys towards war and aggression? Our instincts are to serve all of the community. Our want for more has led to hierarchy and war, which pushed us beyond our basic needs into greed. The best way to raise warriors is to start them with a war-like mentality from birth…. This is the dawn of masculinity.

Which came first - War or Masculinity

Let's take a brief look at a few countries and the roles of men and women in antiquity compared to the roles of men and women after the agricultural and industrial revolutions. The reason for this contrast and comparison is to include a look at how societies were influenced over time and how the roles of men and women changed during these times.

Japan

"Chinese records dating back to the first century reveal that women were not only allowed to rule, but also encouraged to rule due to a confidence in women to bring peace and regulation to the country." In regard to the influence of religion on Japan, Mallary goes on to write, "In 552 A.D., the introduction of Buddhism from China would interfere with the Shinto-dominated perception of women."[34]

According to Dr. Lebra and Joy Paulson, "The aspects of Buddhism which define its character had begun to make inroads on society's attitude towards women." This particular form of Buddhism that was assimilated in Japan was immensely anti-feminine. Japan's newfound Buddhism had fundamental convictions that women were evil, which eventually led women into a submissive role in Japanese society. Regardless of this, women in Japan would find ways to become educated. An example would be Lady Murasaki, who wrote the first Japanese novel, "The Tales of Genji."[35]

Women would find their height of power during the Kamakura period. "Women were playing a more active role in society, reconnecting from behind the Heian barriers. Women even trained in the ways of the samurai."[36] As feudalism progressed, the role of women became constricted and modeled more on the lord and subject. Even more so after the Meiji restoration, where Japan changed from a feudal/samurai class system to a Western monarchy/parliament oligarchical government. As the bushido lifestyle of men in Japan changed from war with swords to war with guns, the industrial revolution was also underway in Japan. The government was setting up vast industries to bring Japan into the future to rival its Western counterparts. Japan also started to set its sights on building an empire. As men went to war or worked in agriculture, women worked in industry as indentured slave labor. Prostitution also became a booming business in Japan. As the birth demand for boys grew, unwanted girls were sent into prostitution. As Japan's Imperialist conquests moved forward, the lives of Japanese women required strength on two fronts: work and home. Men were at war and entrenched in pushing the might of the Japanese Empire. Men were expected to take on their duty and fight to the last breath. There was no place for home in a soldier's heart. This allowed them to distance themselves from the empathetic and emotional part of their souls. This allowed them to commit atrocities against whole countries in Asia that people still recount in horror to this day. Post World War II Japan underwent another push to further industrialization and modernization.

As Japan gained more and more on the economic end, men bore the brunt of the continual work/life sacrifice as salari-men. Work 12 to 16-hour days, 6 days a week, for the sake of the company. The company was the new emperor of Japan, and all workers put their hearts and souls into the company. Women put their hearts and souls into the family. Women were given more freedoms in society, however, this was limited to domestic life. Some women broke the barrier into the Japanese workforce. As time went on, more and more women started to work, and the appeal of marriage waned as freedom and a career could bring. This has much to do with the male-dominating society in Japan. There are stories where men would grope women on trains, sexually harass women. The image of women in society was that of a demure, quiet, reserved woman who does what a man asks of her with no complaints, raises her family and takes care of her husband. This became her duty to society.

For men, toxic outlets to vent their frustration and feelings were needed. Heavy drinking has been the norm, and hostess bars allowed men to be able to speak their feelings, but at the expense of degrading women. Women were seen as objects for men's wants and desires. Sexual Harassment remains a prominent problem for women in the workforce.

Many of us have seen satires written or played out, about Japanese men and how societal norms paved the way for suicide and toxic relationships within families.

To Japan's credit, the old ways of thinking have gradually changed over time; however, the Japanese machine has not been able to change fast enough. As women started working and forgoing marriage, men found themselves purposeless. They had been given empty pitches about what their lives would be like, and that marriage was an expected step in their lives. Women realized it was better to stay unmarried than to be shackled by societal chains of domestication. This is the current state of Japan - declining birth rates, declining rates of marriage, an increasing male suicide rate, increase rate of male loneliness and anger. Women have gained more opportunities in Japan since the introduction of Buddhism and Shintoism decreased their equal standing in ancient Japan. Men, however, are left in a "Purpose Void".

England

During the Upper Paleolithic period, the people of this period, ranging from Cro-Magnon to Neanderthal to Homosapiens, were hunter-gatherers, hunting mammoth and reindeer. They used tools and signals to track the birthing pattern of reindeer. In these hunter-gatherer societies, men and women hunted and foraged for food. The first distinct culture was the Creswellians. They continued the line of hunter-gatherers.

"Food species eaten by Creswellian hunters focused on the wild horse or the red deer. Probably depending on the season, although the Arctic hare, reindeer, mammoth, Saiga antelope, wild cow, brown bear, lynx, Arctic fox and wolf were also exploited."[37] These societies were found to have traded with other groups of people. Note that there is about an 18,000-year gap in the history of England due to the glacial period. The Britons were the first people of England who the Romans then conquered in 1AD. Prior to this, Britons maintained hunter-gatherer societies. Britons moved to a more domesticated lifestyle during the Neolithic Revolution. Agriculture led to larger societies and changes in religion, which are believed to have led to gender roles and social division.

"The traditional view is that agricultural food production supported a denser population, which in turn supported larger sedentary communities, the accumulation of goods and tools, and specialization in diverse forms of new labour. The development of larger societies led to the development of different means of decision-making and to governmental organization. Food surpluses made possible the development of a social elite who were not otherwise engaged in agriculture, industry or commerce, but dominated their communities by other means and monopolized decision-making."[38]

Jared Diamond[39] identifies the availability of milk and cereal grains as permitting mothers to raise both an older (e.g., 3 or 4 year old) and a younger child concurrently, resulting in a more rapid population increase. Diamond, in agreement with feminist scholars such as V. Spike Peterson,[40] points out that agriculture brought about deep social divisions and encouraged gender inequality. Veronica Strang[41] traces this social reshuffle through developments in theological depictions. Strang supports her theory through a comparison of aquatic deities before and after the Neolithic Agricultural Revolution, most notably the Venus of Lespugue and the Greco-Roman deities such as Circe or Charybdis: the former venerated and respected, the latter dominated and conquered. The theory, supplemented by Talcott Parsons's[42] widely accepted assumption that "society is always the object of religious veneration," argues that with the centralization of government and the dawn of the Anthropocene, roles within society became more restrictive and were rationalized through the conditioning effect of religion; a process crystallized in the progression from polytheism to monotheism. This is similar to what took place in Japan, where deities could be female and changed with the influence of religion. The Celtic Britons had a history of warfare among various clans during this time, up until the invasion of the Romans. As Rome declined, the Anglo-Saxons invaded the Celtic Britons and became the dominant group during this time. English history is then dominated by the monarchy, internal and external wars and religion, all taking place up to and including the Agricultural Revolution.

The Agricultural Revolution, 17th to the late 19th century, led to the Industrial Revolution in Britain. The Industrial Revolution set Britain on its path of world conquest and colonialism. The constant war-like state and agricultural revolutions required that men take on the roles of warriors to defend their land and conquer their neighbors. Leaders of these societies were in constant states of war for resources. War became the means of ascension in English society. Feudalism brought about a society where the wealthy would own land and peasants would work on these lands and provide military service for their lords. Men were soldiers, and held a greater degree of power than women, regardless of social class. Throughout English history, men would fight in wars for lords and rulers for the protection of their way of life and society. The life of a soldier has always played a prominent and distinguished role in English society. Men were allowed to change their fates through military service. As the British Empire took over more of the world, the opportunities for men expanded as they subjugated people for the British Crown. For women, their roles would gradually change with religion and agriculture. Early Celtic Briton women were part of an egalitarian society, where they hunted and foraged for food alongside men. As conflicts grew among the Celtic Britons, men and women fought alongside each other. Girls and boys grew up learning how to use weapons. Women and men, even though men were more likely to hold these positions, could be healers and religious leaders. Some Celtic women were, at times, leaders of their communities and armies.[43]

Two famous women are Cartimandua and Boudica. As Rome took over, the rights of women were diminutive in the eyes of the Romans. The Celtic Britons, however, maintained their egalitarian societal views of women. As Anglo-Saxons took over Briton the role of women became more domesticated. Women maintained some of the respect enshrined in Celtic Briton society; however, women were more and more domesticated and confined in British society. Under British Society, the rights of women were dependent on men. Men held legal and magistrative power over women through the family and in marriage. As the industrial revolution picked up and the world was thrust into World War 1 and World War 2, women's rights made greater strides in Britain; in education, labor, and society, all to the point where in 1975 Margaret Hilda Thatcher, or Baroness Thatcher, was made leader of the Conservative Party in the British Parliament and became the Prime Minister of Great Britain in 1979.

As women fought for their freedoms and pushed themselves forward, Britain was also losing its empire. The great British Empire took a back seat to its cousin, the United States of America. The opportunities for societal advancement for men through means as a soldier were no longer available. As Britain turned inwards, the growing influx of foreigners threatened to take the remaining skilled labor jobs available. Britain was able to provide higher education to both men and women; however, women made greater gains in society. Men have higher rates of suicide; lower rates of enrollment in University; a rise in anti-immigrant ideology; misogyny and misogynistic inclinations; the employment rate of men has decreased while the employment rate of women has increased from 1971 to 2022. Men are left in a "Purpose Void".[44]

The United States of America

We now turn our attention to the Democratic Experiment, the United States of America. In order to discuss the United States, we need to look at American history from the establishment of the colonies. Indigenous people and tribes have long and wonderful histories whose potentials had been cut short by colonialism. For this reason, we will start this analysis from the early colonization of America. Early colonial America was founded by religious fundamentalist; the Puritans were victims of religious persecution in England. As every child in the US learns, the Puritans sailed from England to the United States on the Mayflower and landed on Plymouth Rock and settled in the New Land. The Pilgrims celebrated their first harvest with the indigenous people, which was the first Thanksgiving celebration. A Salem Witch Trial here, smallpox outbreak and murder of indigenous people there, expansion of the colonies North and South, then West, throw in some voluntary indentured labor here and involuntary chattel slave labor there, some spilled tea, and a war against Britain, and we come to the part in US history which is the founding of the United States of America. The United States' Bill of Rights was ratified on December 15th, 1791. The Bill of Rights is the name given to the first 10 amendments of the United States Constitution. [45]

It is important to note that when the Constitution was written and ratified, historians widely accepted that it was written at the benefit of men and landowners; subsequent changes to the Constitution have led to it becoming a more inclusive document. Men have benefited greatly from the way the Constitution was written and how the government was structured. It was a government created for men by men. I use "was" to acknowledge that the constitution is not the same document it was at its inception. Over time, women like Elizabeth Cady Stanton, Susan B. Anthony, Sojourner Truth, Ida B. Wells and many others fought for the rights of women to be given the same rights and privileges as men under the Bill of Rights. On August 18th, 1920, the 19th Amendment was ratified, giving women the right to vote. The vote was ratified by 56 senators, two over the threshold needed to approve the amendment. While most women were celebrating the right to vote, men still held on to the original power center in politics and society.

This societal power secured them as heads of the household, protectors and providers for their families. In the years after the 19th amendment, women continued to fight for the rights to join the military, have bank accounts, hold patents and copyrights in their names, own land in their names, engage in larger society, attend primary and secondary schools, as well as attend University. Women could become doctors and lawyers, members of Congress, the Senate and Vice President. All in all, women have been able to close in on the power, economic and social gap between men and women; and with the Equal Rights Amendment, this would have been a constitutional step towards full equality.

Let's discuss the Equal Rights Amendment to give a fuller picture of women's struggles for equal rights. "Three years after the ratification of the 19th Amendment, the Equal Rights Amendment (ERA) was initially proposed in Congress in 1923 in an effort to secure full equality for women. It seeks to end the legal distinctions between men and women in terms of divorce, property, employment, and other matters." [46] In the minds of many, the ERA was not ratified due to the work of Phyllis Schlafly. She was the prominent voice in the 1970s that pushed for states to stop ratification of the ERA amendment; "She argued that the Equal Rights Amendment would eliminate the men-only draft and ensure that women would be equally subject to conscription and be required to serve in combat, and that defense of traditional gender roles proved a useful tactic."[47] The FX TV series "Mrs. America" deals with Mrs. Schlafly's life and activism related to the ERA. The ERA is a critical potential amendment to the US Constitution. The ERA updates the rights and freedoms for all living in America.

Even with the loss of the ERA, women were still able to make great strides in women's rights. American society made great strides to push towards equality for women. As time went on, women in the US began to increase their shares in the number of college graduates, business owners, general and career employment, home ownership, purchasing power, and percentage of wealth in America. Male-dominated parts of society also started to open up to women. Science, Technology, Engineering, Arts and Math (STEAM) programs made great efforts to increase primary and secondary educational enrollment in these programs. Women had also seen an decrease in the maternal mortality rate (with the exception of black women), saw their reproductive rights protected by the Supreme Court for 50 years, and held accountable the people or programs that were responsible for the sexual, physical and psychological trauma inflicted on women in their employment or care. Through all of the gains women have made, more recently, they have had to endure the rise of misogyny and the overturn of 50 years of a woman's right to make choices regarding her health and her body. The decreases in female societal gains followed the rise of misogyny. With this, we have also seen a decrease in male participation in primary and secondary schools, the workforce, and other areas of society. This is part of the *"Boy Crisis,"* which we will speak of later. Women continue on the upward trajectory, and men are reversing course and seeking alternate outlets to vent their frustrations. Their anger is towards the changing dynamic of a world where they were told to be protectors and providers, and find a world where there is no longer a need for these singular roles. The domineering role of men that was once a hallmark of American society is no longer. Men are left in a "Purpose Void."

These related societal themes of egalitarian to hunter-gatherer to agriculture to the separation of roles for men and women follow the same template in many societies. The roles of men as protector, provider, and soldier; and women as domestic, mother, and nurturer, echo throughout human history. The power dynamic between patriarchal-defined gender definitions has improved for women and is in the process of evolving for men. For men to be successful in our changing society, the definition of masculinity has to change, as does society's view of men and masculinity.

Chapter 2 Summary

Masculinity didn't drop out of the sky, it was built over thousands of years as humans shifted from egalitarian hunter-gatherer bands to agricultural, hierarchical societies first for resources and then control. As agriculture, surplus, and static land took hold, war became the main tool for protecting and stealing those resources, and men—the physically stronger sex, less tied to childbearing—became the perfect weapon, rewarded with power, status, and women while women were pushed into second-class roles. By tracing Japan, England, and the United States, I show the same pattern repeating: religion, empire, industrialization, and law all reinforcing male dominance, then slowly expanding rights for women, until men's old roles as warrior, sole provider, and unquestioned leader started to collapse. What we're left with now is a generation of men in a "purpose void," watching women gain ground while the old scripts for manhood no longer work. This chapter sets the historical baseline: masculinity as we know it is a product of war, hierarchy, and power—not destiny—and if it was built, it can be rebuilt.

Main Points

- Early human societies were largely egalitarian, with flexible roles for men and women; hierarchy and patriarchy emerged as agriculture, resource concentration, and ownership created power imbalances.

- War and male physical advantages turned men into the primary tools of violence and resource acquisition, hard-coding masculinity to dominance, protection, and control while pushing women into second-class status.

- Across Japan, England, and the United States, industrialization, empire, and women's rights reshaped gender roles, leaving many modern men in a "purpose void" and showing why masculinity as we inherited it must be redefined.

Chapter 3

Masculinity and the woman who defined it

Now that we have primed the conversation, it is important to understand and be aware of the link between agriculture and the rise of power - the need and want for additional resources, war, and its tie to masculinity. Let's define masculinity based on a widely accepted psychological masculinity and femininity test. These are a series of personality trait tests designed to describe a person's degrees of masculinity and femininity based on societal standards. Some of the tests include, but are not limited to, the Minnesota Multiphasic Personality Inventory, the Guilford–Zimmerman Temperament Survey, and the Gough Femininity Scale. For this book, I am choosing the Bem Sex Role Inventory because it also includes androgyny, which is a space between masculinity and femininity. It is a word that captures the idea that we can encompass multiple traits and should be judged not by our appearance but based on our character and how we treat other humans. I believe this plurality of traits is needed to effectively save ourselves, as individuals, and as a species.

We cannot discuss the Bem Sex Role Inventory (BRSI) without first acknowledging that it has its critics and is more of a historic model. Other tests perform similar functions and meet the current needs of today. The purpose of using this test, in this discussion, is because of its legacy use as it relates to the historical context used in this book in defining the idea of "masculinity." It is important that you also take the test to get a better understanding of where you would stand on the BRSI scale and keep that in mind as you continue to read this book. Continue to question yourself, your ideology, your belief systems, as well as the concepts in this book. If you would like to know more about current gender identity research, please read review concepts like the Gender Identity/Gender Expression measures, the Gender Self-Definition and Self-Acceptance Scale, or other qualitative/experience-based approaches.

In 1974, American psychologist Sandra Lipsitz Bem created the Bem Sex Role Inventory or BRSI. The American Psychology Association defines the Bem Sex Role Inventory as "a questionnaire listing 20 characteristics considered in American society to be more desirable for men (e.g., leadership ability, forcefulness), 20 characteristics considered more desirable for women (e.g., gentleness, affectionateness), and 20 neutral characteristics considered desirable for either sex (e.g., truthfulness, happiness)."[48]

"Participants indicate how well each of the 60 characteristics describes themselves using a scale ranging from 1 (never or almost never true) to 7 (always or almost always true). Responses are scored and individuals subsequently categorized as masculine (high on traits associated with masculinity and low on those associated with femininity), feminine (high on traits associated with femininity and low on those associated with masculinity), androgynous (high on both types of traits), or undifferentiated (low on both types of traits). In measuring a person's adherence to culturally specified standards of desirable behavior for men and women (see sex role), the BSRI was intended to eschew the traditional dichotomy of masculinity and femininity in favor of a more flexible, situationally responsive conceptualization." [49]

When I took the test, I received the following scores:

[Dean,] (y)our scores on the Bem Sex Role Inventory are as follows:

Ratings rank from 1 to 7, with a mean of 4

- Femininity: 5.0

- Masculinity: 5.05

- Neutral items: 4.9

Interpretation:

- If both your Femininity and Masculinity scores are above 4, you are 'androgynous'.

- If both your Femininity and Masculinity scores are below 4, you are 'undifferentiated'.

- The neutral items are not further interpreted.

The Psytoolkit.org provided the following disclaimer regarding the results:

"There are different ways to do the scoring. Therefore, you are recommended to read the papers on the PsyToolkit library website.

Note that the interpretation is not generally accepted and that there has been a lot of debate about it. Also, it is culture-specific, so please be cautious with the interpretation.

Finally, this PsyToolkit questionnaire has been sorted by scale, whereas it might be better to mix them all randomly."[50]

As a reminder this test is being used as an example for foundational understanding purposes.

Masculine and Feminine Traits

What are the traits that are considered masculine and feminine? The images below[51] are taken from the BSRI-12, which is the 12-item version of the Bem Personality Test.

Figure 1. BSRI-12 Items

<u>Feminine</u>	<u>Masculine</u>
Warm	Has leadership abilities
Gentle	Strong personality
Affectionate	Acts as leader
Sympathetic	Dominant
Sensitive to other's needs	Defends own beliefs
Tender	Makes decisions easily

Figure 2. Bem (1974) Gender Roles

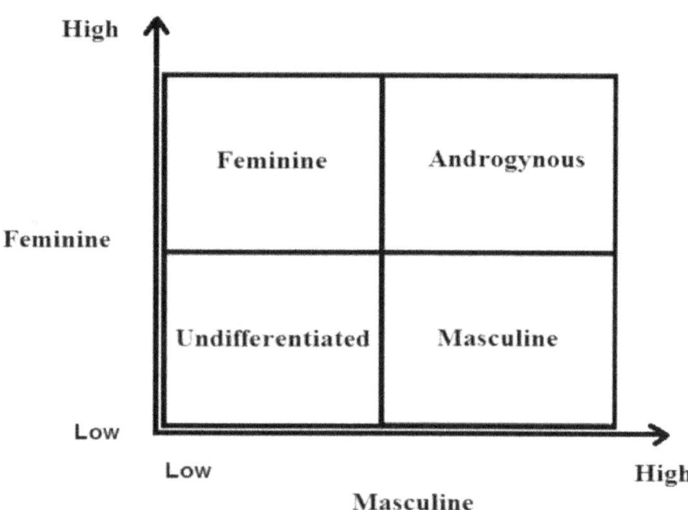

Let's review each of the traits included under masculinity:

Leadership abilities

> *Before you are a leader, success is all about growing yourself. When you become a leader, success is all about growing others.* - Jack Welch

> *A leader is a dealer in hope* - Napoleon Bonaparte.

The word leadership is from Old English laedere "one who leads, one first or most prominent," agent noun from laedan "to guide, conduct. In the article "What is Leadership", Alberto Silva notes the following as a summary of the definitions: "For many centuries, leadership was seen just as a personal quality. Confucius, the great Chinese thinker who lived about 2,500 years ago, did not propose any definition of leadership but insisted on the need for leaders to be virtuous and look after the people around them. For him, a leader's primary purpose is to serve the people. For Plato, who many recognise as the founding father of philosophy, the leader should be wise.[52]

Machiavelli stated that the leader should have good virtues and should be intelligent to have the support of the people.[53]

In the 19th century, Thomas Carlyle, a 19th century Scottish Historian and social critic, summarized the recurring ideas about leadership in his theory of the "great man."[54] For him, leaders were exceptional persons or heroes who were able to use their charisma, intelligence, wisdom, and political skill to have power and influence over other people. Although Carlyle's ideas remained predominant, Spencer pointed out that such great men were the products of their societies or the context, anticipating the modern debate about leadership." [55]

Taking responsibility and ownership for one's actions is another point of leadership. We are also advised that leadership has societal and cultural definitions and is not gender specific. Many of the books that I have read on leadership lend themselves to the notion that a leader is responsible for the outcome of any and all situations under their leadership. In "Extreme Ownership: How U.S. Navy SEALs Lead and Win", the authors write ", On any team, in any organisation, all responsibility for success and failure rests with the leader. The leader must own everything in his or her world. There is no one else to blame. The leader must acknowledge mistakes and admit failures, take ownership of them, and develop a plan to win." [56]

Based on this legacy definition of masculinity, leadership abilities would mean that a person can use charisma, intelligence, wisdom, political skill, have good virtues, be moral, be a guide, and look after the people around them and in their community.

Strong Personality

No one cares how much you know until they know how much you care. - Theodore Roosevelt

What is a strong personality? Can it be considered a relative term? Is the Alpha in one pack seen at the same level as the Alpha in another pack?

First, I want to talk about this Alpha and Beta male syndrome that varying groups in our society seem to be obsessed with. The traditional definition of "Alpha male" is that they are the dominant males in a group with access to more or most of the resources, like food and mating access. Beta males are the subordinates or males of the groups that do not have similar access. There is also a mindset that alpha males are the leaders of the pack. So let's look at the question - do wolves have Alpha and Betas? Yes, but only in the way that I, as a child, was the beta to my grandmother or mother. That is what an Alpha and Beta relationship is to a wolf pack. The alphas of a wolf pack are the elders of the pack, and a female can be an alpha.

Let's look at this further: there is strength of personality and strength of character. A strong personality is where a person is able to use various attributes like build, vocalization, intelligence, physical prowess, etc., to obtain resources. These strong personalities may take from the group for themselves to ensure that their genetic line survives. This may be the definition of an Alpha male, but will this type of person serve the "pack" in a social hierarchal society? Strength of character would be linked more to a person's ability to continue when their chips are down or when those around them have given up. Character is a trait that people can rely on in their evaluation of a person. Their character, if known, precedes them and factors into how society interacts with them – can they be trusted, will they do what is right, can I rely on them to be there in my time of need? The biblical characterization of Job, who lost everything God had given him and was tested by the Devil to forsake God, is an example of character. All through the strength of his character, he was able to hold firm in his belief. A personality that relies heavily on physical strength fades. Our bodies fail us, our minds fail us, but our character endures and truly leads. Our character defines our destiny and who we are remembered as when we pass.

Strength of character does not mean that a person is of moral or amoral character. Strength of character means that the person is more able to use their given natural talents and abilities to guide an individual or group along the path of their plans. This is more the definition of a strong personality. It is a hybrid of our previous definition of personality and character.

One of the defining characteristics of a strong personality is emotional intelligence. Emotional Intelligence is a person's ability to empathize with others and make them feel and believe that their life, ideas, choices, and opinions matter to the observer. Dale Carnegie's book "How to Win Friends and Influence People"[57] is a modern-day hack to understanding people and gaining emotional intelligence. A person with a strong character can show their strength in multiple ways. Donald Trump is a person with a strong personality, and would easily be added to the list of people mentioned in the song "Cult of Personality" by Living Colour.[58] Obama, Dr. King, Oprah, Gandhi, Stalin, Hitler, Reagan, General Patton, Bernie Mac, Richard Prior, Michael Jackson, President Truman, Putin, Chancellor Merkel, John Wayne, Jackie Robinson, David Bowie, Prince, Michael Jackson Clint Eastwood, Lucille Ball, Koffi Annan - each of these people have or had strength of personality, regardless of our thoughts about their moral leanings.

Their strength was through their intelligence (emotion or traditional) or a projection thereof. Their natural abilities, whether through their swagger, grit, charisma, effective communication, etc., create an aura of strength and magnanimity that affects the people in their charge.

Acts as a leader

How is "Acts as a leader" different from "Has leadership abilities?" All of us have some form of leadership ability. Many of us are intelligent, have charisma, have moral standing, and support from our friends and families. We meet or exceed the definition of "strong personality." At times in life, in the course of business or social order, we may be given the opportunity to have power and influence over people. "Acts as a leader" is the difference between having leadership skills that may be reflected in "strong personality" and using them. Leadership abilities can be gained over time. It's similar to the power-ups in the old video games like "River City Ransom", where you can go into a store and buy a book to increase your fighting strength or learn a new move.

I have spent years reading books that I thought would give me leadership abilities. I've read books by John C Maxwell, one of the leading authors, on leadership. I've read books written by former Navy Seals and Generals, and I have read books that discuss how people think and why we do what we do. I have read books on procrastination and time management, and books about how to have conversations and make friends. I have even read books written about General Patton and his take on leadership. I believe many of these books have been helpful in my continued evolution. With all of this knowledge gained, I still would not consider myself a leader. Leaders have continual moments of leadership. The actions of a leader make a leader. When I have had leadership roles, I understood that those were just titles. I once thought that the title of leader would make me a leader. A leader understands when to apply their abilities for the benefit of those who have entrusted them with power. A leader is also able to see a wide path forward and the steps ahead, all to help their team see and understand the right actions for success. A leader knows when to push, when to pull, when to start, when to drop, when to support, and when to let lead. In my role as President of the Harlem Rotary Club, I have applied many of these skill sets and worked towards being a better leader each day.

Dominant

I would like to think it means "to have dominion over oneself and the things you do"; however, dominant means "most important, powerful, or influential." Dominant is to be able to bend situations to your will. Dominant can also be tricky to define because dominant is a trait that can be quantified as well as qualified. If there are 100 times more men than women in a group, then men dominate. They dominate by sheer numbers. Their dominance is quantified. If the women are the best female track stars in the past 50 years, and the men are randomly selected off the street to have a race against the women, then we can make a qualified statement that the women dominate the men in track. In society and some cultures, the presence of a man would dominate the group. Wonder Woman in a group of superheroes is dominant, even with Superman present (no letters please.)

The quantitative nature of dominance allows for a superiority in numbers, which can be projected as qualitative. The United States does not have an advantage over North Korea in terms of the number of soldiers; in this way, North Korea dominates with pure numbers. Militarily, the United States' military dominates the North Korean military based on firepower and military might. Why speak of this in terms of the military?

Dominance is a word that invokes the sense of conflict, regardless of whether or not there is one. In genetics, the dominant trait is expressed over the recessive trait. The dominant figure is able to have their point of view expressed over the lesser. Dominance allows a person or group to shape the worldview and thinking of others. Dominance uses fear as the catalyst to exert pressure to force others to conform, as it relates to social and political interactions.

Defends Own Beliefs

This is an interesting concept. I don't think it's much of a stretch to say that all people defend their beliefs; however, the concept is assigned as a masculine trait. In this day and age, with misinformation abounding, we need to first look at how this would have looked 40 + years ago when the BRSI was created. At that time, we did not have the news silos and information bubbles we have today. With a limited selection of news sources, many of us shared the same facts with our neighbors and within our communities. So why would beliefs need to be defended? Most likely, beliefs related to religious, cultural and societal differences would need to be defended, not current affairs or news related items.

In the defense of one's beliefs, a disposition develops. This disposition can be physical or intellectual. Men are seen as having higher intellectual prowess than women. Debating was, at one point, an overwhelmingly male endeavor. Reason is a tool that was believed to be found only in the arsenal of men. Men can debate and explain the logical validity of their beliefs, and many would follow that belief. With masculine traits being interwoven in conversation, masculinity is able to project dominance and leadership qualities to appeal to others during the defense of their belief. If "reason" fails, then physical threats can also play a role in the defence of one's beliefs. I believe x because of y and will defend my belief by any means necessary, either through physical/mental fortification or physical/mental confrontation. In the defense of a belief, the other party is either for you or against you.

Makes decisions easily

The pattern of masculinity is one perfect circle where each part relies on the other. When making a decision, there is a clear outcome. If you look at a decision tree or logic diagram, you get an idea of a person or group's decision-making process as well as their internal thought process. This process includes the question posed, the final decision and the paths taken to get to the final desired outcome. Some decisions are made by looking at multiple outcomes and decision variables. General Patton was known for his great decision-making process - "The time to take counsel of your fears is before you make an important battle decision. That's the time to listen to every fear you can imagine! When you have collected all the facts and fears and made your decision, turn off all your fears and go ahead!"[59] He was known to gather his lieutenants and painstakingly go through each battle scenario, and when they came up with a plan of action, it was the only plan. All contingencies were accounted for, and all confidence came from the plan.

One subject that I have found of great interest is Game Theory. Game Theory is a system that works to find the best outcome for a situation. In the movie "War Games," the protagonists taught the computer to play

Tic Tac Toe as a last-ditch effort to prevent nuclear annihilation; it did not understand the no-win scenario. In Star Trek, the Kobayashi Maru is a leadership test and simulation of a no-win situation. It is designed to teach humility and introspection after loss. Captain James T. Kirk was the only person to win the "no-win" scenario by reprogramming the computer. The masculine mindset that there is always a way to win; there's always a solution - a winner and a loser, is prevalent in this moment. This drives the decision-making process. There is no compromise, only finality.

While growing up, I always thought of a leader as someone who had no flaws and was always cool under pressure. I grew up watching movies where the good guy was the one person who stood up to the bad guy and would lead the people to safety. The leaders of corporations and countries were hard men who would quash dissent among their ranks. In my youth leadership, duty and honor came in the forms of TV icons like Optimus Prime, Duke, Al Bundy, and real-life icons like my youth pastor John Noel, Dr. Martin Luther King, Abraham Lincoln, my grandparents, teachers and mentors. As I got older, I began to understand more about the reality and nuances of life and the decision-making process. I began to understand that leaders are people who get scared, but do what is necessary for the good of the people.

I realized how much more difficult the choices these leaders make are, in spite of their character flaws. Leaders I admired began to evolve and include people like Former Presidents Jimmy Carter and Barack Obama, General George S. Patton, Former Secretary Hillary Clinton, Arizona Senator John McCain, Former Congresswoman Liz Cheney, Kofi Annan, Nelson Mandela, Greta Thunberg, and many other leaders who have decided to take the road less traveled. They made the hard choices when it mattered, for the greater good.

In modern definitions of masculinity, you may find words like Emotional Intelligence, Gender equality, self-awareness and personal growth, strength and resilience, authenticity and individuality. Emotional Intelligence, self-awareness, and personal growth would be covered under "Leadership Skills'' within the Bem Sex inventory; Strength and resilience would be covered under dominance; Authenticity and individuality would be covered under "Defends one's beliefs." Gender Equality is an interesting add, but it is subjective.

There are many thoughts on gender identity and gender roles. Equality itself is an interesting term. To become equals. Some see gender equality as men and women making the same amount of money for the same job, and the erasure of stigma and the patriarchy that has kept women from equality. Based on this book, I would extend that to also add that there are men who also want to erase the patriarchy. To many men, masculinity has become a millstone around our necks. Men should also want equality for women to help reduce the societal pressures that both genders face day to day. I believe that any call for equality should include metrics that qualify the efforts towards equality, and also discuss how society moves forward once these metrics are met.

The male and female genetic conjunction – More Science

I want to share an interesting conversation I had with a couple who have become my adoptive parents, regarding the relationship between War and Masculinity. My "Playa Mom and Dad" recently came to visit my daughter and me in New York City. I first met them in 2017 at Burning

Man, where I was introduced to the ideas of enthusiastic consent and empathy—concepts that were already widely discussed within the burner and alternative lifestyle communities. Burning Man and the journeys thereafter were my introduction and subsequent adaptation of these principles. Mom and Dad were discussing the topic of this book with me, and Dad said he believes that there is a genetic component to war. He believes that masculinity is not the result of war, but is more an inherent part of who we are as humans. Men are better adapted for war and are thus better suited and capable of the act (I discuss this in the section "How Men are the perfect weapon"). So the question remains: is there evidence of humans, or our nearest evolutionary relatives, going to war for reasons outside of the need for resources? Some studies support both sides of the argument.

Dr. Alex J Bellamy[60] , in his article "Humans may have evolved aggression, but that doesn't mean we were hard-wired for war," states that war was not evident in human civilisation prior to 10,000 BCE. After this time, there is evidence of gated structures built to keep out invaders and death from wars. In Scientific America a year earlier, Brian Ferguson, in his article "War is *Not* Part of Human Nature" (emphasis the author's), wrote the following introduction: "Do people, or perhaps just males, have an evolved predisposition to kill members of other groups? Not just a capacity to kill but an innate propensity to take up arms, tilting us toward collective violence?" [61] The word "collective" is key. People fight and kill for personal reasons, but homicide is not war. War is social, with groups organized to kill people from other groups.

Today, controversy over the historical roots of warfare revolves around two polar positions. In one, war is an evolved propensity to eliminate any potential competitors. In this scenario, humans, all the way back to our common ancestors with chimpanzees, have always made war. The other position holds that armed conflict has only emerged over recent millennia, as changing social conditions provided the motivation and organization to collectively kill. The two sides separate into what the late anthropologist Keith Otterbein called "hawks and doves."

"The basic Hawk-Dove model imagines a scenario where two alternative strategies for contesting resources are subject to selection. The hawk strategy is to always fight and only retreat if an injury is received. The dove strategy is to use an agonistic signal against other doves and to always retreat from hawks. On the face of it, playing hawk might seem better, but when we consider the outcome of each possible combination of hawk and dove, we see that this will not always be the case. Doves will always lose when playing against a hawk, but they can expect to win half of the contests they have against other doves.

Furthermore, doves never get injured. Hawks always win against doves, with no risk of injury, and on average will even win half of their contests against other hawks. The downside of playing hawk is that in half of the contests that they lose to other hawks, they receive an injury. Thus, while the benefits of the resource are important, so too are the costs of fighting." [62]

So the question then becomes, have evolutionary pressures forced us to become doves or are we hawks? Evolution pressures toward survivability. There is also a version of this game theory that plays out with a retaliatory dove. In that scenario, the retaliator comes out on top. Game theory is a very interesting field of study and can be applied in many situations in life. It teaches us how to evaluate the potential cost of a decision. If war expresses an inborn tendency, then we should expect to find evidence of war in small-scale societies throughout the prehistoric record. The hawks claim that we have indeed found such evidence. "When there is a good archaeological picture of any society on Earth, there is almost always also evidence of warfare...Twenty-five per cent of deaths due to warfare may be a conservative estimate," [63] wrote archaeologist Steven A. LeBlanc and his co-author Katherine E. Register. With casualties of that magnitude, evolutionary psychologists argue, war has served as a mechanism of natural selection in which the fittest prevail to acquire both mates and resources. This perspective has achieved broad influence.

Political scientist Francis Fukuyama wrote that the roots of recent wars and genocide go back tens or hundreds of thousands of years among our hunter-gatherer ancestors, even to our shared ancestor with chimpanzees.

Bradley Thayer, a leading scholar of international relations, argues that evolutionary theory explains why the instinctual tendency to protect one's tribe morphed over time into group inclinations toward xenophobia and ethnocentrism in international relations. If wars are natural eruptions of instinctive hate, why look for other answers? If human nature leans toward the collective killing of outsiders, how long can we avoid it? The anthropologists and archaeologists in the Dove Camp challenge this view. Humans, they argue, have an obvious capacity to engage in warfare, but their brains are not hardwired to identify and kill outsiders involved in collective conflicts. Lethal group attacks, according to these arguments, emerged only when hunter-gatherer societies grew in size and complexity and later with the birth of agriculture. Archaeology, supplemented by observations of contemporary hunter-gatherer cultures, allows us to identify the times and, to some degree, the social circumstances that led to the origins and intensification of warfare. [64]

Richard W. Wrangham in his article "Two Types of Aggression in Human Evolution" and his book "The Goodness Paradox: The Strange Relationship Between Virtue and Violence in Human Evolution" writes about the two types of aggression that have influenced human history "Two major types of aggression, proactive and reactive, are associated with contrasting expression, eliciting factors, neural pathways, development, and function. The distinction is useful for understanding the nature and evolution of human aggression. Compared with many primates, humans have a high propensity for proactive aggression, a trait shared with chimpanzees but not bonobos. By contrast, humans have a low propensity for reactive aggression compared with chimpanzees, and in this respect, humans are more bonobo-like." [65]_[66]

In The Goodness Paradox, Richard Wrangham argues that humans have undergone a process of self-domestication marked by reduced reactive aggression. As anthropologist John Hawks notes in his commentary, this process resembles the selective breeding for tameness seen in Dmitry Belyayev's fox experiments, an idea that can be traced back to early speculations by Johann Friedrich Blumenbach in the early nineteenth century. The debate still rages on with tests that have shown that aggression can be genetically altered in mice; however, behavior in humans tends to be both genetic and environmental. A great example of this is the neuroscientist Dr. James Fallon, who found out, during his research on psychopaths, serial killers, schizophrenics and depressives, that he has the genetic markers as well as the brain scans of a psychopath. The Smithsonian magazine published an article about this titled "The Neuroscientist Who Discovered He Was a Psychopath."[67]

"One afternoon in October 2005, neuroscientist James Fallon was looking at brain scans of serial killers. As part of a research project at UC Irvine, he was sifting through thousands of PET scans to find anatomical patterns in the brain that correlated with psychopathic tendencies in the real world. "I was looking at many scans, scans of murderers mixed in with schizophrenics, depressives and other normal brains," he says.

"Out of serendipity, I was also doing a study on Alzheimer's and as part of that, had brain scans from me and everyone in my family right on my desk." "I got to the bottom of the stack, and saw this scan that was obviously pathological," he says, noting that it showed low activity in certain areas of the frontal and temporal lobes linked to empathy, morality and self-control. Knowing that it belonged to a member of his family, Fallon checked his lab's PET machine for an error (it was working perfectly fine) and then decided he simply had to break the blind that prevented him from knowing whose brain was pictured. When he looked up the code, he was greeted by an unsettling revelation: the psychopathic brain pictured in the scan was his own."

Dr. Fallon[68] has also written a book titled "The Psychopath Inside", in which the Doctor discusses how he was able to have a normal family and life even with this diagnosis.

The science is currently inconclusive as a sole determining factor. Our genetics and environment play important parts in nurturing our nature. This is why it is important to understand how men are nurtured in our society, and how this gives way to who men are expected to be, who we are, and what we want to be.

Another factor in the tale of male and female behavior is estrogen and testosterone. The NIH's website provides the following definition of Testosterone and its use: "Testosterone is a sex hormone that plays important roles in the body. In men, it's thought to regulate sex drive (libido), bone mass, fat distribution, muscle mass and strength, and the production of red blood cells and sperm. A small amount of circulating testosterone is converted to estradiol, a form of estrogen. As men age, they often make less testosterone, and so they produce less estradiol as well. Thus, changes often attributed to testosterone deficiency might be partly or entirely due to the accompanying decline in estradiol."[69] What about estrogen? What is the purpose of Estrogen? "Here are the major roles estrogen plays in women's health:

- *"Puberty and sexual development:*
  Estrogen is responsible for the development of your reproductive system. The anatomy of your vagina and uterus is dependent on this busy hormone. Pubic hair, the hair under your arms, and the development of your breasts are all thanks to estrogen.

- *Menstrual cycle:*
  Having your regular monthly period may not always be fun, but it's a positive sign of your health as a woman and your ability to conceive a child. Estrogen builds the lining of the uterus in

anticipation of pregnancy. If no pregnancy occurs, estrogen enables you to shed the lining of your uterus via your period.

* ***Healthy bones:***

The development of your bones is owed to estrogen. As you age, estrogen works to protect your bones against loss of mass. Once you enter menopause and your estrogen production decreases, the loss of bone mass increases. You become at-risk for osteoporosis, which can lead to fractures, severely impacting your quality of life and healthy ageing.

* ***Healthy heart:***

You may be familiar with post-menopausal women who are on hormone replacement therapy in an effort to protect their cardiovascular health. That's because once menopause hits and your estrogen levels drop, your risk for heart disease goes up. Estrogen plays a major role in heart health. This helpful hormone keeps blood vessels healthy and pliant, controls cholesterol, and prevents increased inflammation, a huge threat to heart health.

* ***Your mood:***

Estrogen boosts the production of the brain chemical serotonin. Serotonin balances your mood. That's why, when estrogen levels drop, in postpartum or menopause, many women suffer from depression."[70]

It was noted earlier that men also produce estradiol, which is a form of estrogen. The types of estrogen and their roles are as follows:

"Depending on your season of life, your body produces different types and amounts of estrogen in an effort to maintain balance."[71]

The types of estrogen and their primary function are:

Estradiol: Also known as E3, it's present in women between puberty and the onset of menopause. The amount your ovaries produce can go up or down, depending on where you are in your menstrual cycle.

- ***Estrone:***

  Also known as E1, its present in its greatest amounts during those same childbearing years as estradiol. During that time, it's second only to E3 in amount produced. Although production diminishes after menopause shuts down your ovaries, it's still produced by your body to a small degree.

- ***Estriol:***

  The pregnancy, estrogen is produced to support the placenta and fetal development.

So, what does Estradiol do to men, even at low levels, and do women produce testosterone? If so, then how does it affect them?

Let's look at Estradiol:

"Estradiol in men is essential for modulating libido, erectile function, and spermatogenesis. Estrogen receptors, as well as aromatase, the enzyme that converts testosterone to estrogen, are abundant in the brain, penis, and testis, organs important for sexual function. In the brain, estradiol synthesis is increased in areas related to sexual arousal. In addition, in the penis, estrogen receptors are found throughout the corpus cavernosum with high concentration around neurovascular bundles. Low testosterone and elevated estrogen increase the incidence of erectile dysfunction independently of one another. In the testes, spermatogenesis is modulated at every level by estrogen, starting with the hypothalamus-pituitary-gonadal axis, followed by the Leydig, Sertoli, and germ cells, and finishing with the ductal epithelium, epididymis, and mature sperm. Regulation of testicular cells by estradiol shows both an inhibitory and a stimulatory influence, indicating an intricate symphony of dose-dependent and temporally sensitive modulation. In women, testosterone also plays an important part, similar to the role Estradiol plays in Men." [72]

The effects of healthy testosterone levels in women are felt throughout their bodies:

- ***Reproductive tract.***

  Androgens, such as testosterone, influence female reproductive functions, including the ovaries, uterus, vagina, and clitoris. In early follicular development, receptors are located on various ovarian cells. As such, dysregulation of testosterone may upset normal reproductive development.

- ***Circulatory system.***

  Testosterone plays an important part in red blood cell (RBC) formation, also known as erythropoiesis, and helps protect women against anaemia, a condition characterised by insufficient supplies of RBCs or oxygen-carrying haemoglobin.

- ***Muscles and bones.***

  Testosterone is believed to increase bone mass and periosteal bone formation. Results of two studies employing testosterone implants in addition to HRT showed noteworthy positive effects on bone mineral density. The hormone also helps increase muscular growth and maintain muscle mass.

- *Breasts.*

  For women suffering from a testosterone deficiency, research suggests that treatment with testosterone (hormone therapy) could prevent proliferation of estrogen cells in the breast, thus decreasing breast cancer risk.

- *Skin.*

  Healthy testosterone levels in women contribute to greater skin collagen content and thickness. This is especially evident in menopausal women, whose skin collagen content has been found to decline due to lower testosterone and estrogen levels.

- *Brain.*

  Research suggests that testosterone helps prevent Alzheimer's disease because it modifies brain structures, particularly the hippocampus, which is responsible for the formation of one's memory. Studies show that women with sufficient testosterone levels have improved spatial memory.

Both Testosterone and Estrogen play important roles in regulating pivotal functions in their respective bodies. I have read arguments about the influence of testosterone on men and the relation to aggression and sex drive. Men do have higher sex drives than women. This fits within the scientific consensus. Both men and women use these hormones to regulate their bodies, and they can both be found in increased and decreased concentrations in an individual's body for various reasons. A person should not be reduced to the difference in their body's hormonal balance. It is important to understand those differences and treat each person with respect and empathy.

To close this section, I will point to a double blind study where the participants were given testosterone. This was to test how testosterone affected the participants. This is their abstract, "Although in several species of birds and animals, testosterone increases male–male aggression, in human males, it has been suggested to instead promote both aggressive and nonaggressive behaviors that enhance social status. However, causal evidence distinguishing these accounts is lacking. Here, we tested between these hypotheses in men injected with testosterone or a placebo in a double-blind, randomized design. Participants played a modified Ultimatum Game, which included the opportunity to punish or reward the other player. Administration of testosterone caused increased punishment of the other player, but also increased reward for larger offers. These findings show that testosterone can cause prosocial behavior in males and provide causal evidence for the social status hypothesis in men." [73]

In reading the study, you find that the participants with increased testosterone would select outcomes that would increase or defend their role in the social status. They were aggressive to be protective, but would be aggressive in the reward-giving as well. Further study is required; however, it does give pause to the thought that testosterone is all downside because of the aggression that comes with it.

Chapter 3 Summary

Masculinity, as we've inherited it, is a constructed system built from psychological tests, cultural expectations, and a long history of assigning traits to men that were never biologically exclusive. I introduce the Bem Sex Role Inventory not as gospel, but as a legacy tool that helps us see just how arbitrary many of our ideas about "masculine" and "feminine" traits really are, and why androgyny offers a healthier, more flexible way to understand ourselves. From leadership to dominance to defending beliefs, I break down how these traits became coded as masculine, even though history, psychology, and lived experience show they belong to all humans. I also examine the biological side—testosterone, estrogen, genetics, and evolutionary debates—to make one point clear: biology influences us but does not excuse or define us. Ultimately, this chapter challenges the reader to question old narratives, understand the blend of nature and nurture shaping behavior, and recognize that redefining masculinity starts with honest self-examination rather than clinging to outdated scripts.

Main Points

- Masculinity, as traditionally defined, is not innate—it is a cultural construction shaped by psychology, social expectations, and historical power structures.

- The Bem Sex Role Inventory (BSRI) offers a legacy framework for understanding how society assigns "masculine" and "feminine" traits, highlighting the value of androgyny and the limitations of rigid gender categories.

- Biology, hormones, and evolutionary theories interact with but do not dictate male behavior; environment and social conditioning play equal or greater roles in shaping what we call "masculinity."

Chapter 4
Mad Men, Modern Day Men,
and the "Boy Crisis"

I.   *What is the measure of a man? Who was, who is, and what will he be?*

The age of "Mad Men", as coined in the TV show of that name, has ceased to exist. The lone man suffering in silence goes and seeks vengeance for the less fortunate.

John Wayne, James Dean, James Caan, Wesley Snipes, Arnold Schwarzenegger, Sylvester Stallone, Dolph Lundgren, Mr. T, Hulk Hogan, Michael Jordan, Clint Eastwood, Bruce Willis, Clark Gable, Lawrence Taylor, Wilt Chamberlain, and others, similar in character, are all men who fit the masculine profile. These are all men, who at some point, fit the mold of the masculine narrative - "Has Leadership abilities, Strong personality, Acts as leader, Dominant, Defends own beliefs and Makes Decisions Easily." These are all men who had public personas that men could look to and see masculinity play out on the big and small screens. This masculinity is then used by advertisers to sell their products, using the needs for sex and acceptance through masculinity to pull men's attention to their products.[74]

In wrestling, the term *Kayfabe* "is the portrayal of staged events within the industry as 'real' or 'true', specifically the portrayal of competition, rivalries, and relationships between participants as being genuine and not staged. The term kayfabe has evolved to also become a code word of sorts for maintaining this "reality" within the direct or indirect presence of the general public."[75] Each of these personalities, at one time or another, was considered the pinnacle of masculinity. They were leaders in their individual professions, and they were dominant in character. They would defend their beliefs as they aligned with their professional or public persona. They were seen as men of action. The other part that isn't said out loud is the sex and misogyny that their characters played to, on or off the set. Not every person lived up to this lifestyle of excess and masculinity, hence the use of the word Kayfabe. These men lived their lives in the service and agenda of money. The man who can increase a company's profitability became the definition of masculinity during that point in society's Overton Window.[76]

Men have been systemically conned into a belief of what masculinity is, how we should behave as men, and what is within our "rights" as the "dominant" member of our species. All done in the name of financial gains for some and a fake bill of goods, filled with dreams of a future of sex and "alpha dominance" for those taken in by the con. The result of this Kayfabe is generations of men who were taught to push down their feelings and needs; they were taught to disregard the emotional baggage and "emotional damage" caused by the falsehoods in society's definition of masculinity. At the beginning of each generation, before they are given the millstone of masculinity, lie our boys, open and ready for life, ready to take on their purpose. We must not fail them.

A. The "Boy Crisis"

In 2018, Dr. Warren Farrell wrote a book titled "The Boy Crisis: Why Our Boys are Struggling and What We Can Do about it.'" [77]

In 2022, Richard V. Reeves wrote "Of Boys and Men: Why the modern male is struggling, why it matters, and what to do about it." [78]

And before them all, Christina Hoff Sommers wrote "The War against Boys: How Misguided Policies are Harming Our Young Men" in 2000, which was updated in 2013. [79]

These books are at the forefront of the conversation regarding the "Boy Crisis." I will use these books as the foundation and cornerstones of the remainder of this book. There will be other books and media discussed during this phase of the book, ranging from Josh Harwley's book "Manhood: The Masculine Virtues America Needs," [80] "Self-Made Man" by Norah Vincent, [81] Andrew Tate videos, Reddit subreddits like Two X Chromosomes, various channels on Clubhouse, YouTube and other areas of the internet where the conversation about masculinity has taken shape and is being discussed.

The path taken from the start of this book to now - from introduction, critical thinking practices, to the history of humanity and agriculture, to the physiology and psychology of masculinity- is all part of a broader discussion within the halls of literature and media. The purpose of masculinity doesn't jump off the page immediately. My goal is not to convince you with overwhelming evidence. My goal is to help facilitate discussions about how we can take back our humanity and our roles in society as men and redefine the narrative of masculinity in society. As a side note, I highly recommend reading each of these cornerstone books to get a better understanding of the context and concepts of this book. Of the three, I would recommend starting with "The Boy Crisis."

One of the first ideas that struck me during my research was that of the "Purpose Void". The "Purpose Void" is the loss of purpose that men were faced with as more and more women were taking up the mantle of breadwinner. Dr. Farrel writes that a male's purpose has been that of breadwinner, warrior, protector. The role of breadwinner is diminished in a two-income home. With the rise of divorce, increased education, and increased pay, women have the means to go it alone in this world. It does not mean they want to, or even have to; it does mean that the factors for domestic cohabitation have changed. A man's paycheck and purchase ability no longer sway the conversation of what a successful man is. Unfortunately, men have been programmed to believe that their main objectives in life are to be the breadwinner and protector of their family and communities. Women, for the most part, are able to protect themselves and their children. Female empowerment has helped contribute to the increase in gun ownership and rise in self-defense courses in America. Protection and self-defense are no longer seen as male-centric. With the loss of his purpose and without gaining a new one, the current generation of men cannot pass on their purpose to the next generation of men.

There is an entity that corporations and governments use continuously to instill the trope of what masculinity looks like, and this is set upon each successive generation: advertisement. As women made economic gains, advertisers would pivot their focus on female empowerment to ensure they claimed their share of the new female markets. These commercials moved women from the role of homemaker to that of corporate risk taker; from buxom blonde waiting for a man to tell her his needs and desires, to bosses in pantsuits and heels commanding and leading men. Commercials for men continued to focus on sex, trucks, beer, and the essence of all that defined masculinity. This is the same masculinity that has dominated humanity from the start of the agriculture period and continues to this date. War. Sex. God and Country. To advertisers, Men are walking penises that have been programmed to aim their attention towards the manipulated masculine fight of the day. The fight against Socialism, Communism, Gay and Lesbian Rights, Climate Change, etc. Without a purpose, it is easier to guide those young male minds, to move them away from education and pull them away from the world. These young men wake up to find out that the bill of goods they were sold wasn't worth the paper it was written on. This is the "Boy Crisis".

What are some of the impacts and/or causes of the *"Purpose Void"*? What are some of the male perspectives:

- **Education** - "For every 100 bachelor's degrees awarded to women, 74 are awarded to men."[82] More and more men are opting out of education, and the traditional factory jobs or trades schools are becoming increasingly the only option to get into the middle class.

  The male perspective: I cannot take on the role of breadwinner that has been ingrained in me from the time I was a child. I cannot be what society has expected of me because society has turned its back on me and my educational needs. My emotional needs, during my school years, are not even in the public consciousness. I do not matter.

- **Social** - Young men are pulling away from society and becoming insular and anti-feminist, which is referred to as "Incels". There is a growing number of men and young boys who believe that the women's rights movements have taken away their natural place in society as the dominant figures in both the home and greater society. "Women have lost their 'softness' and their need for men." Men, in turn, have lost access to being the pillar to the quintessential roles that women have played for generations, that of child bearer, child rearer and wife.

  The male perspective - Society has, in order to advance equal rights, pushed to provide more girls and young women with options towards educational and financial success. At the same time, while society was keeping track of where women were achieving, society stopped working to maintain the benchmark levels in boys and young men. This bias has weighed heavily on the masculine self-image and their understanding of their place in society.

- **Wages** - "The wages of most men are lower today than they were in 1979, while women's wages have risen across the board."[83] There is a justified discussion ongoing regarding the gender pay gap, in which studies show that the full story needs to be further evaluated and explained to the general public. There is a pay gap; however, factors including traditional job types and the types of roles that have been historically stereotyped as male or female roles are factors in the pay gap.

  The male perspective - Without an education, it isn't easy to take on the middle-class lifestyle. At one point, it was easier to make it into the middle class with a trade or factory job, but those jobs are no longer available or diminishing. Even when looking for work or entering into a traditionally female job, we face bias and prejudice there as well. We may want to be teachers, nurses, or caregivers, but there is a perception that, as a man, I am incapable of the empathy and warmness required for these roles, or that I am a sexual deviant swayed by my lust and thirst for power.

- **Fatherhood** - "One in five fathers are not living with their children."[84] The trend of fathers not showing up and being responsible for their children is on the downswing. Fathers want to be included in the lives of their children; however, society and the legal system are still set up in ways that default to the mother in many areas regarding child rearing. The laws are getting better; however, this is a continued struggle for men.

  The male perspective - I want to be a father to my children; however, I am unable to find consistent work, and if I do have a consistent job, the courts diminish my role as father, and they side with my child's mother. I also have to contend with the effects of my child being told untruths about me and who I am in an effort by others to create a gap between me and my children. I am not given enough time with my child to imprint on them. The only part of me that survives in my child is my genes, not my love, not my essence. Nothing of me will exist beyond my life.

- **Mental** - Men account for almost three out of four "deaths of despair," [85]either from a suicide or an overdose. Society's continued image of what masculinity is has fostered the image that men are more capable of containing their emotions and can control them in a cold, calculating way. A real man is able to cope silently and swallow their pride to do the thing they must do in order for their family to survive. This in turn has led to increased suicide rates in men. Talking to a psychiatrist, or even friends, about one's feelings is seen as a sign of weakness and an effeminate trait in men. Some women have been known to perpetuate this idea of masculinity and would look down upon a man for his sensitivity and vulnerabilities. I stress that this is not all women, but more a general understanding and experience that many men experience.

The male perspective - I have to be tough and strong and carry through no matter what. I cannot afford to look weak. The pain and stress are unbearable at times, and I don't know where to go. Drugs and alcohol only lead me to greater depression. I am trapped with no way out….. But one. I think everyone will be better off.

- **Masculinity** - Toxic masculinity is a topic that could probably go under the anti-feminist and Incel argument; however, there is more to it. Toxic masculinity is a by-product of unchecked, misguided and sometimes misunderstood masculinity by men. This correlates further with mature and Immature Masculinity. Some say that not every voice needs to be heard. If the point of reconciling our humanity is to be inclusive, then all voices should be heard. We cannot continue to isolate a group from society because their thinking does not align with ours. Creating paths to fruitful exchanges of ideas and fostering empathy and understanding are the ways to humanism and understanding.

Male perspective - This is how men have behaved for years and how we are conditioned to behave to keep in line with society's definition of masculinity. I play the role that they have defined for me. I need to show my masculinity to protect myself from the pain that exists in my heart, in the life I have lived as a man and to protect myself from the toxic masculine display of others. My strength is the only true power that I have, and I must wield it to show that I exist.

These are some of the arguments that are the backbone of the "Boy Crisis".

The next step is to take a deeper look at each argument and review how each author discusses and addresses these issues, as well as their respective solutions, where available. We will then review how these solutions tie back to redefining masculinity, along with mature and Immature Masculinity.

As with every section of this book, I want the reader to take a few minutes and think about the message and the feelings that evolve when reading this book. Are you challenging yourself and your way of thinking about this topic? This book is not to shame or deflate men. This book is a way to help and save men. Save their humanity and save humanity as a whole.

Education

As a child, my grandmother always taught me the importance of an education. She told me that an education is the one thing no one can take from me. My grandmother is a product of the Jim Crow South. She was a single mother who went to school to become a nurse and also received two Master's Degrees. She also volunteered for the Red Cross and was awarded the Ann Magnuson Award. She is an example of the many who have been able to improve their lives with an education.

An education has historically been one of the assured paths to the middle class in America. The higher you go in your education – grade school, middle school, high school, or college, the better your chances of successful entry into the middle class. In the United States, public education is a relatively recent idea; in fact, this is the case in most of the world. At one point, one could become a lawyer or doctor through trade practice alone. As time went on, these professions required a greater degree of education. Abraham Lincoln is probably one of the better well known persons who would become a lawyer as an apprentice.

For years, men were better educated because they were expected to be the breadwinners in the home and the patriarchy. Women were educated in the domestic arts of keeping a home. Ironically, Abraham Lincoln's mother also ensured that he had a domestic education as well. Over time, more women from wealthy families were able to enroll in higher education. The push for public education had a greater impact on income, racial and gender inequalities. As societies began to create laws and programs that created a form of equal access to education for all, there was a greater emphasis on equality and equal opportunities for women and minorities. Many of these policies were well-intentioned, but without clear metrics, regular check-ins, and the flexibility to adjust when results fell short, the balance quickly tipped out of scale.

Christina Sommers, in her book *" The War Against Boys: How Misguided Policies are Harming Our Young Men,"* lays some of the blame for the *"Boy Crisis"* in education at the feet of one Professor Carol Gilligan. Ms. Sommers believes that Ms. Gilligan and others have written about the failure of girls to achieve success in their education careers. In her book,

Ms. Sommers does a good job of countering this narrative. She writes, in *The War Against Boys* (2000), Christina Sommers recounts how women's organizations anticipated a landmark Department of Education study that they hoped would validate claims that girls were being shortchanged in American schools. The movement, influenced by figures such as psychologist Carol Gilligan, relied heavily on subjective studies about self-esteem and classroom dynamics rather than on measurable academic outcomes. Works like Mary Pipher's *Reviving Ophelia* reinforced the narrative that girls were emotionally and academically endangered during adolescence. [86]

However, when the Department of Education's *Trends in Educational Equity* report was released, it told a different story. Using federal data on grades, test scores, and college enrollment, researchers found that girls were not falling behind but, in many respects, outperforming boys. Roughly half of the study's forty-four indicators showed no gender difference; a few favored boys in math and science performance, but overall, girls had stronger grades, greater literacy skills, and higher rates of college matriculation. As the report's director, Thomas Snyder, noted, the results revealed that "the female advantage in school performance is real and persistent," a finding that surprised even those compiling the data.

The argument she makes here is that young girls were doing better than the *"short-changed girl's movement"* would lead us to believe. In the last part of the paragraph, Ms. Sommers does acknowledge the gender gap in math and sciences persists; however, she chalks this up to a gender bias towards boys liking math and science. Has this trend persisted?

In *Of Boys and Men* (2022), Richard Reeves explains that girls have long excelled academically, and their advantage has grown most sharply in reading and language skills. He notes that this divergence begins early: by kindergarten, girls are about fourteen percentage points more likely than boys to be "school-ready," even after adjusting for family background. This readiness gap is wider than those tied to income, race, or preschool attendance. By fourth grade, girls lead boys in reading proficiency by roughly six points, and by eighth grade, that difference almost doubles. In math, boys hold a slight early edge, but it nearly disappears by middle school. Drawing on national test data analyzed by Stanford researcher Sean Reardon, Reeves reports that female students outperform males in English-language arts in nearly every U.S. school district—the average gap equaling about two-thirds of a grade level, a difference larger than most educational interventions achieve. Reeves includes a figure summarizing this pattern: when high-school GPAs are ranked from lowest to highest, girls cluster strongly toward the top deciles while boys appear more often in the lower ranges. Together, these findings illustrate a durable academic imbalance now favoring girls across nearly every educational measure.[87]

During the course of reading these books, I also wrote my own comments and notes. These are the basis for my commentary throughout. I ask that you do the same for this book for future community discussions and reviews. Based on Mr. Reeves' information, the trend in academic success for grade school girls has increased, and girls have overtaken boys in every education metric. This has led to a decrease in the number of young men entering college, to the point where being a male applicant at a college is a factor in admission. Potential female applicants take the male-to-female ratio into consideration when deciding on which schools to attend. I will point out the irony of how a push towards equality through the selection process has created a preference for males in the college selection process. This can even be extended to racial diversity. More and more students consider racial diversity when selecting a college or University.

In *The Boy Crisis* (2018), Warren Farrell expands on the growing discussion around boys' educational struggles. He notes that worldwide, reading and writing—the two skills most strongly tied to later success—are also the subjects where boys lag furthest behind. In the United States, by eighth grade, roughly 41 percent of girls are considered proficient in writing, compared to just 20 percent of boys. Farrell connects this widening gap to a generational shift in motivation. In the past, many young men became focused during high school as they anticipated becoming family breadwinners—a role that once provided pride, purpose, and direction. With that expectation fading, academic engagement among boys has declined, leading to a drop in male college completion from about 61 percent to a projected 39 percent. Farrell also highlights research showing that boys who perform equally to girls on standardized tests often receive lower grades in the classroom, suggesting that behavior and conformity influence evaluation more than ability. Boys who act in ways traditionally perceived as "feminine," such as being quiet or eager to please, are graded more favorably, while those displaying "boy-style" energy are penalized. This, he argues, contributes to many boys' growing disinterest in school and perception of bias against them. [88]

The theme of boys doing better in subject areas they like and the downturn in their grades in other courses could be a correlation. Ms.

Sommers also writes a similar line in her book regarding how the qualities of being a boy are used against them in school and play a factor in the overall education of boys.

> "We have turned against boys and forgotten a simple truth: the energy, competitiveness, and corporal daring of normal males are responsible for much of what is right in the world. No one denies that boys' aggressive tendencies must be mitigated and channeled toward constructive ends. Boys need (and crave) discipline, respect, and moral guidance. Boys need love and tolerant understanding. But being a boy is not a social disease." [89]

I disagree with the alignment of behavior with gender as a major factor, as I will show later, there are environmental and genetic factors involved as well. One topic that all three writers discuss is the increased diagnosis of boys with Attention Deficit Hyperactivity Disorder. Each writer has their own take on why the diagnosis is increasing, as well as their respective solutions. Historically, there was a time when boys did better than girls in school settings. What was the change that occurred where the behavior of boys became a challenge in executive function? Has there been research to determine if there is a correlation between teaching styles and or teaching practices and the increase in ADHD diagnoses? I would also point to another culprit, which Dr. Farrell and Ms. Sommer do point to…. teacher expectations. One famous study is the *Pygmalion Effect* by Rosenthal and Jacobsen,[90] which showed that a teacher's bias towards the perceived intelligence of a student would affect the student's grades overall. More research on teacher behavior and teaching styles is needed to provide further data to help prepare real-world, effective solutions.

As a young man growing up in Brooklyn, I was fortunate enough to have the experience of going to both public and private schools. I was not a particularly disruptive child until junior high school, which correlated with the time of my continual sexual assault. In grade school, I went to private schools; we seldom had disruptions in class, and if we did, the punishment was a ruler to the open hand. Particularly nasty infractions got a rap on the knuckles with said ruler, and "capital punishment" would be either the belt, administered by the Pastor or the science teacher. I have experienced Pastor level administration, but never science teacher-level. I don't think my frail frame would be able to handle it. I can't honestly say if the physical punishment worked better. When I was in Junior High School, I would get pre-suspended each year without fail. Disappointing my grandmother brought more pain than anything. I did conform under physical punishment, but disappointment had a deeper feel to it. She had to leave work to meet with the Dean of Students.

I was a better student at the private school; however, I was facing demons of my own during junior high school and acted out as an effort to keep my feelings internal. In reflection, I believe that having the ability to express myself and/or having access to counseling would have been a greater help for me and other students who faced challenges similar to those that I faced. I know that I am not the only voice that resonates with this. There are husbands, fathers, partners, and sons who have felt this overwhelming sense of emotionality. The only way we can express ourselves is in ways that keep our masculinity intact - hence the high-risk, high-reward behavior. All done to be seen for who the world wants us to be, so we, in turn, are seen. Sometimes society is lucky enough to find these young men and help them to be who they can be. To help them become unburdened by masculinity. Unfortunately, others get lost and drowned in the viscosity that is toxic masculinity.

Suppose we are aware of the growing trend towards educational malaise in boys and young men. Are we also aware of the potential effects that these lost generations will have on humanity's future?

The potential outcomes could look like the following:

1. **Education**

   As men leave school behind, the salary potential that comes with education also decreases. If more women are getting their degrees and moving into the middle class, women may have fewer partners to select from if they are looking for someone of equal earning potential.

2. **Labor**

   Manual labor or trade jobs, typically sourced by immigrants, will compete with the domestic workforce. This becomes even more prescient with AI poised to eliminate many entry level white collar jobs. The job pool for manual jobs will increase while jobs decrease. This may also play into a positive effort of increasing the dating pool once manual jobs are more in demand than mid to senior level white collar jobs that AI can perform.

3. **Family**

   The "Dropped out Left out Cycle," As described by Dr. Farrell[91]

   a. "In neighborhoods where marriage is scarce, fathers are scarce, and more than half of boys don't finish high school. The boy drops out.

b. The less education a young man has, the more likely he is to be unemployed or underemployed. He's left out of the workplace.

c. Women who desire children think of an uneducated young man as undesirable, and an unemployed man as "another child"—hardly marriage material. He's left out of marriage and fathering.

d. Some of the women with whom he nonetheless has sex become pregnant and raise children without him. Thus, we're back to step one: the left-out dad and the drop-out son."

4. Bias

We could end up losing the male perspective. There is a potential bias towards male vs female students, which is being further studied. Male students who have more qualities associated with femininity - patient, subdued, polite, to name a few- are better able to gain a teacher's favor than their counterparts. Boys then lose interest in school once they realize no one is paying attention to them and their needs. Studies have shown that a diverse workforce is the best type to have. This goes for education as well. Being able to listen to the opinions of people from varying backgrounds, positions in life and culture, as well as sex, adds to the overall efficiency and output of any process. Christine Sommers writes, "But what is hard to understand is why the math and science gap launched a massive movement on behalf of girls, and yet a much larger gap in reading, writing, and school engagement created no comparable effort for boys."[92] Great efforts have been made to help girls achieve parity in Science and Math, and the question is valid in relation to the same effort towards boys.

5. Anger and Resentment

We could end up losing men to the appeal of misogyny. An educated class is more able to use critical thinking and be in touch with their humanistic and empathic abilities to work together and find compromise. Without the bias checks enacted by education and empathy, men could turn to creating harmful and repressive systems of control to eliminate gains made by women and control any future paths of progress. The "Handmaid's" tale is a perfect example of a system put in place to benefit men. When the Taliban took over Afghanistan, women lost most of the rights they had gained through the US occupation. Many thought the Taliban would allow for some of the gains made by women to remain in place. As of this writing, most or all of these gains are gone.

6. Economics

As of 2017, the poverty rates between men and women in the US were as follows:

- 10.9% for men and 13.6% for women;

In the year 2018, the rates were:

- 10.6% (-.3%) for men and 12.9% (-0.7%) for women.

Looking forward to the year 2021, we find the following rates:

- 10.3% (-0.3%) males and 12.6% (-0.3)females in 2020 and

- 10.5% (+0.2) for males and 12.6% (-/- 0.0%) for females in 2021.

The data shows a modest narrowing of the gender poverty gap, with women's rates declining slightly faster than men's. Pandemic-related income disruptions in 2020 temporarily increased poverty rates, so multi-year data will be needed to determine whether this shift persists.[93_9494]

Youth are the greatest group impacted by poverty.

Poverty rates range from 17.4% and 16.2% in 2017 and 2018, respectively, to 16% and 15.3% in 2020 and 2021. That is a - 2.1% decrease from 2017 to 2021.

In the preceding years, the rate of graduation from college was 33.2% male and 33.7% female in 2016, to 33.7% (+0.5%) male and 34.6% (+0.9%) female in 2017.

In 2019 and 2020, we see rates of 35.4% (+0.8%) males and 36.6% (+2.0%) females, and in 2021, 36.6% (+/- 0%) males and 39.1 % (+2.5%) females. [95]

We would need to continue reviewing these trends to determine whether there is a connection between poverty rates, graduation rates, and employment levels among men and women. The numbers tell one story at a glance, but as with all data, context matters. There are also more women in the population than men, which has to be factored into any interpretation. If we were to look at the percentage of children under eighteen living in poverty and compare that to the percentage of men and women graduating from college, we could reasonably hypothesize that women may be moving out of poverty at a faster rate than men, especially when considering the decline in poverty among women over the same period. Still, it would be faulty science to claim that the numbers alone prove this out. Reality is never that simple. Additional research and deeper analysis are needed before concluding. Scientists, economists, and policy analysts are studying these patterns, trying to make sense of what the data truly show—and more importantly, to find ways to bring those numbers into balance through education, opportunity, and societal change.

7. Behavior and Bias

The last factor is the increased diagnosis of ADHD (Attention Deficit Hyperactivity Disorder) in boys than in girls, as well as the stigma this plays in a child's development. The underdevelopment of the prefrontal cortex causes ADHD This is the area where executive function takes place. Executive function is another word for impulse control. Children with ADHD are often unable to control their impulses and "act out" based on this lack of impulse control. The prefrontal cortex in humans does not fully develop until the age of 25; however, in children with ADHD, their prefrontal cortices are not developed in tandem with other children their own age. The current thinking, in regards to the increase in diagnoses in boys vs girls, leans more towards a misdiagnosis of ADHD in girls. Girls do not show the same signs of ADHD as presented in boys. Part of the reason is the role that gender identity plays in how boys and girls interact. Boys are taught, at an early age, that their rambunctiousness and carefree attitudes are how boys are supposed to act or play out. Mrs. Sommers speaks about this quite frequently in her book. [96]

Girls are usually taught that this type of behavior is not acceptable for a girl, and they learn to suppress or limit how their impulse control is expressed through their "play" behavior.[97] Teachers and parents know better what signs to look for in a boy, as they relate to ADHD, than they would in a girl. A similar issue is girl-on-girl bullying, which is underreported yet is prevalent in the lives and upbringing of girls in today's society. Dr. Farrell also discusses a potential link between ADHD to a child's diet, which I will discuss further in the solutions section. [98]

Chapter Summary

In this chapter, I examine how modern masculinity was shaped, marketed, and ultimately narrowed into a performance that rewarded dominance, silence, and economic output while discouraging emotional awareness and adaptability. The masculine archetypes many of us grew up with, reinforced through media, sports, and advertising, offered a clear script for what it meant to be a man. That script once served a purpose, but society changed while the narrative did not. What remains is a version of masculinity that no longer aligns with modern life, yet continues to be imposed on boys and men with real and lasting consequences.

At the center of this discussion is what has come to be known as the "Boy Crisis." Drawing from the work of Farrell, Sommers, and Reeves, I explore how shifts in education, labor, family structure, and gender roles have disrupted the traditional sources of male purpose without offering meaningful replacements. The result is not simply frustration or confusion, but a generational loss of direction. Boys are growing into men without a clear understanding of where they belong, how they contribute, or why they matter.

Education emerges as one of the clearest warning signs. Boys are falling behind across nearly every academic measure, not because they lack intelligence or capability, but because the systems meant to support them increasingly reward behaviors misaligned with how many boys develop, learn, and express themselves. When this educational disengagement is paired with economic instability, reduced access to fatherhood, stigmatization of vulnerability, and unresolved definitions of masculinity, the consequences extend beyond individual men. This chapter is not written to assign blame, but to surface patterns, question assumptions, and prepare the groundwork for redefining masculinity in a way that restores purpose, humanity, and shared responsibility.

Main Points

- **Masculinity Has Been Performed, Not Inherited**

  Cultural archetypes of masculinity were manufactured through media, advertising, and economic incentives, encouraging men to suppress emotion and equate worth with dominance and productivity. This performance, sustained through social reinforcement and profit motives, left little room for emotional development or adaptability, setting the stage for long-term harm.

- **The "Purpose Void" Is Central to the Boy Crisis**

  As traditional roles such as sole breadwinner and protector diminished, men were not given new, equally valued purposes. Without a clear path to meaning, boys disengaged from education, community, and self-development. This absence of purpose now manifests in academic decline, social withdrawal, resentment, and increased deaths of despair.

- **Educational Systems Reflect Bias, Not Neutrality**

  Boys' struggles in education are not solely behavioral or biological but are influenced by teaching styles, expectations, and institutional incentives that increasingly favor compliance over engagement. When boys feel unseen, mislabeled, or disposable, they opt out. Addressing this imbalance is not about reversing gains made by girls, but about restoring balance, empathy, and effectiveness for all students.

Chapter 5

Solutions to the "Boy Crisis"

The solutions proposed to the "Boy Crisis" are the first steps to redefining masculinity. I believe that the solution to the "Boy Crisis" requires a two-pronged attack. First are direct solutions - Education, Fatherhood and Mentoring, and Mental Healthcare; the second is Redefining Masculinity - how we represent ourselves in our daily lives and society. Each area of the "Boy Crisis" and its respective solution will cover each of the following areas to provide a more all-encompassing solution - Societal, Behavioral, Communal, Technological, and Environmental, where applicable. In some instances, these areas may overlap. Each of these solutions is based on my research and life experience, and I strongly believe that these should be seen as foundational solutions that can be built upon to make things better. Please read this as the beginnings to a solution and not the final solution. The final solution requires involvement from all stakeholders in our society.

So what are the solutions? Reeves believes that boys should start school one year later than girls. Sommer believes that same sex classes, discipline, and cultivating classes around boys' interests are the answers. Dr. Farrell believes that nurturing and educating boys to improve their EQ (Emotional Quotient) and empathy to prepare for jobs of the future that require caregiving. He also believes in taking more time with boys to teach them soft skills and allowing them to be soft without societal stigma attached. Dr. Farrell, Mrs. Sommers, and Mr. Reeves all believe in improving the educational system to incorporate more trade schools. [99]

This is a complex question that requires a strong collaborative effort with social and behavioral sciences, government policies, society, education systems, and economic markets. By using business models that incorporate quality assurance and quality control techniques, we can design systems that are able to improve in real time, based on the current needs, while improving the whole system with the use of monitoring points. Communication is the key element in being able to solve many of these factors. We have the communication techniques and tools needed to obtain data points in real time and we have the means to create these systems. We also have years of research on each factor, along with modeling techniques that can help create specialized solutions for many of these challenges to education. We have artificial intelligence to help craft ways to use or find data that we may not have thought of, along with finding hidden correlations and solutions. This is where we need men and our allies to help push forward and help implement these ideas to find viable solutions. There is a missed opportunity cost associated with the continued decline in the male identity. We need to make sure these costs are discussed and acknowledged to help society and humanity understand the seriousness of the threat we all face from this decline.

Education

Societal and Behavioral

The world as a whole is its own society with a base of behavioral and societal patterns that are unique to the evolution of Homo sapiens. Within each continent, each country, each town, each city, we have developed highly specialized cultures and behaviors that vary in their uniqueness and impact on the boys in these societies. Many times, a society may not be aware of the effect it is having on the larger population until the outliers come to the surface and are then normalized. Once a problem is normalized, it becomes harder to fix because we, humans, do not like change. The adage that a frog would be boiled alive, as the water temperature slowly rises, is a myth. Once the temperature reaches beyond its pain threshold, adaptive abilities, it will jump out of the water. Humans are similar. [100]

We do not always recognize change immediately unless we are already sensitive to a particular change. In the U.S., Irish and Italian immigrants were prejudiced against during the turn of the 20th Century. At this time, there were class distinctions amongst whites that became a barrier to success. As these groups made inroads in American society, they then became "white." Prior to this, if an Irish or Italian immigrant moved into a neighborhood, the neighborhood would get together and decide on how to "stop" this migration before more immigrants came into the neighborhood. As the Italians and Irish became "White," the retribution and disdain of Italian and Irish immigrants decreased.[101]

The Overton Window of immigrant acceptability changed. The concept of social acceptance can change to accept ideas that were previously unimaginable. Italians and Irish became socially accepted as White, even though nothing changed in their DNA. Behavior can also lead to social change. Behavior that was once deemed moral at one point in history is no longer considered moral at present. It is important to acknowledge the term Presentism, which is where we apply our current moral system to events in the past.[102] We lose the lessons in humanity when we do this. It is important to understand that we, more than likely than not, would have had a similar moral code as the people in those days, pending how and where we were raised. We take away the merits of the outlier when comparing it to our current morality. It is important to understand how people can hold a belief and change their beliefs as their moral compasses change.

In education, there is a lack of funding for education as a whole. The baseline for any societal change in education is funding. Our society has to put a greater value on our future and invest in the children we leave behind to forward humanity's progress. How does an increase in funding effect schools? Great Question. The meta-data study "The effects of school spending on educational and economic outcomes" shows the positive impact that more funding has on students. "Event-study and instrumental variable models reveal that a 10 percent increase in per-pupil spending each year for all twelve years of public school leads to more completed years of education, higher wages, and a reduction in the incidence of adult poverty." [103] Increased funding can also be used to add more psychologists and psychiatrists in the school systems to help gain better insight and understanding into what students are facing in today's world, and to take those data points to find effective solutions that can be used to customize the mental health plan for all students. The data points may be able to help point out students in need of help and steer them to safety.

Boys and Girls should have the opportunity to receive the same quality level of education and be free and clear of any harm or bullying in doing so. Dr. Farrell speaks of "poking fun as a way for boys and men to determine whether or not they can trust you with their lives.[104] In classrooms all around the world, boys and girls bully each other. Boys are known more for physical and verbal bullying, and girls more for verbal and social bullying, which makes it more difficult to pick up.[105] I am a victim and witness of bullying and can give a firsthand account of what bullying does to a boy. We learn as young boys to "suck it up" or give back as much as we get. On my bus to middle school, we had a "fight pit" in the bus. There was a boy I fought with two or three times because of the jokes he made about me (they were actually pretty clever). The Brooklyn code was that if someone disrespected you or your mother, you threw hands. With hindsight, I should have let it go and not bothered with what he or others said, but this is how many boys grow up. Millions of boys suffer through bullying in silence, and an unfortunate number lash back in extreme forms of violence. I was lucky in that when I was bullied, it was only in school. I didn't have to go home to view my social media with posts that continued the bullying culture. [106]

The correction for this starts with society and the notion that aggressive behavior is boy behavior. No human should be a victim of inhumane treatment. Our society sees this as a path to education for boys about the real world and teaches them how to be tough, aggressive and protectors. Not all masculine qualities are the qualities needed for tomorrow. It is society's responsibility to prepare our young people for the world of tomorrow. Violence, aggression, fear, insecurity, hate, pain, and self-doubt are a few of the traits that arise from bullying. This is a system that has to be stomped out, starting from the first day to the last day of school. Boys are humans first and should be treated as such. We have the technology and research data to find the most effective ways to teach boys how to effectively communicate their needs and wants to each other and their guardians. This is another avenue that society has to put money into, along with school counseling programs, which will help make a difference to both train and correct boys in the path forward.

In her book *"The War Against Boys: How Misguided Policies are Harming Our Young Men,"* Christine Hoff Sommers writes about scientific studies relating to single sex classes. She does make an effort to show varying views on the effort; however, I believe there is a strong bias towards same sex or single sex schooling. [107]

The debate over single-sex education remains unsettled. Historically, elite single-sex schools such as England's Eton and Harrow have been associated with high academic achievement, but critics argue that their success reflects parental wealth, institutional resources, and faculty quality rather than the single-sex model itself. A more rigorous test came in 2012, when researchers from the University of Pennsylvania examined schools in Seoul, South Korea. Until 2009, Seoul assigned students randomly to single-sex or coeducational schools, providing an unusually controlled environment for study. After accounting for factors like teacher quality, class size, and economic background, the researchers found that students in single-sex schools earned higher college entrance exam scores and were more likely to attend four-year universities—results the authors described as "substantial." Still, the broader body of research remains mixed. A 2005 U.S. Department of Education review found contradictory evidence across studies and concluded that the effectiveness of single-sex schooling could not be decisively proven or dismissed. The Department called the findings "equivocal," noting that the issue may never be resolved through quantitative data alone because it touches on deeper questions of educational philosophy, parental values, and social worldview. If that is so, then the matter would seem to be ideally suited to practical experience, individual circumstance, and voluntary choice.

I recommend that the reader review this subject in more detail and make their own conclusion based on the current scientific consensus. One study I recommend is a 2014 meta-analysis titled "The effects of single-sex compared with coeducational schooling on students' performance and attitudes: a meta-analysis" by Erin Pahlke, Janet Shibley Hyde, and Carlie M Allison.

In the 2014 meta-analysis by Janet Shibley Hyde and colleagues at the University of Wisconsin–Madison examined data from 184 studies involving 1.6 million students in 21 countries were examined to test whether single-sex education improves academic outcomes. The research compared single-sex and coeducational environments across a range of measures, including mathematics and science performance, self-concept, and educational aspirations. While studies without random assignment showed small advantages for single-sex settings, those with stronger controls for selection effects found little to no difference. In controlled studies, the performance gaps were minimal—roughly one-tenth of a standard deviation for math and science—and, in some cases, slightly favored coeducational schools. The authors concluded that, when study quality is taken into account, there is no compelling evidence that single-sex schooling provides measurable academic benefits for either gender. Claims that such schooling particularly benefits minority boys in the United States could not be evaluated due to the lack of rigorous data. This study, which analyzed data from 1.6 million students across 21 nations and a range of income levels, found no meaningful advantage for single-sex education over coeducation. The researchers reported very small effect sizes—represented by the statistical value "g"—indicating that the differences between single-sex and coeducational outcomes were negligible. In short, the data show that separating boys and girls does not significantly improve academic performance. Yet the debate persists.[108]

So why the ongoing push for single-sex education? My hypothesis is that it reflects something deeper than pedagogy. When we separate boys from girls, we preserve the traditional masculine and feminine identities that have long defined gender roles. In doing so, we may also be preserving the archetype of the boy as soldier—conditioned for battle, expected to protect, praised for endurance, and rewarded for emotional restraint. Societies built on conflict have always required such men: strong, silent, and ready to give their lives for causes that often serve only the powerful few. Their bodies and spirits become the currency of ambition, sacrificed for progress that is rarely shared equally.

ADHD or Adult Deficit Hyperactivity disorder is a disorder that affects the prefrontal cortex. The National Institute of Health describes it as "Attention-deficit/hyperactivity disorder (ADHD) is marked by an ongoing pattern of inattention and/or hyperactivity-impulsivity that interferes with functioning or development. People with ADHD experience an ongoing pattern of the following types of symptoms:

- Inattention means a person may have difficulty staying on task, sustaining focus, and staying organized, and these problems are not due to defiance or lack of comprehension.

- Hyperactivity means a person may seem to move about constantly, including in situations when it is not appropriate, or excessively fidgets, taps, or talks. In adults, hyperactivity may mean extreme restlessness or talking too much.

- Impulsivity means a person may act without thinking or have difficulty with self-control. Impulsivity could also include a desire for immediate rewards or the inability to delay gratification. An impulsive person may interrupt others or make important decisions without considering long-term consequences."[109]

Dr. Farrell speaks more about this in his book and discusses alternative ways to treat ADHD through diet and exercise. It is important to understand that this condition is manageable and requires additional funding for diagnosis, treatment and destigmatization. I was once bullied by a co-worker in regards to ADHD. Someone left a highlighted WebMD printout for ADHD on my chair when I arrived at work in the morning. ADHD has always been something I have been conscious about; however, the more research I have done, the more I realize the extent of the stigma associated with it and how varying and severe the conditions can be. Without treatment, you have little control over the greater afflictions of an individual's ADHD diagnosis.

As of this writing, there have been some additional updates on the studies showing new ways that may be effective treatments for ADHD. In the study "Meta-analysis of the efficacy of digital therapies in children with attention-deficit hyperactivity disorder," A new and emerging form of non-pharmacological therapy known as prescription digital therapy is in the preliminary phase of development. According to the definition provided by the Digital Therapeutics Alliance, digital therapeutics (DTx) "deliver medical interventions directly to patients using evidence-based software therapeutic interventions to treat, manage, and prevent a broad spectrum of diseases and disorders." [110] The interventions can be a standalone software program or a program used in combination with self-help therapies such as exercise therapy or dietary therapy, or with hardware-assisted therapies, including neurofeedback training. For ADHD treatment, different digital therapeutic strategies have been designed to improve impairment in cognitive functions or attention control found in ADHD. In 2020, the U.S. Food and Drug Administration (FDA) formally approved EndeavorRx (AKL-T01), the first video game delivered through a video game-like interface for at-home play for the treatment of ADHD in children aged 8–12 years. In a proof-of-concept study, attention and memory performance were improved significantly in patients with ADHD who received this therapy, and minimal adverse events occurred."[111]

There is an expansive treasure trove of studies and information regarding the treatment of ADHD. Two concerns that I think are important to bring up are the racial and pharmacological (or "Big Pharma) bias that comes along with the diagnosis and recommended treatments of ADHD, in addition to the male bias. This is why diversity and inclusion committees must be included in the bodies that approve scientific studies. If the public can be involved and informed at the beginning of a study, the results will reflect the public more and any concerns or potential conspiracies can be addressed in the beginning before testing is done.

Prior to leaving the social and behavioral solutions, I wanted to include a brief discussion about fathers and their relationships with their children. Our society should put a greater emphasis on the importance of raising children, rather than having children. There is a masculine pride in virility in social media. A man with 6 children with 3 mothers will find it very difficult and almost impossible to have a full and loving relationship with each of his children. Children desire their parents' attention, and that attention gets even more divided when there are more parents and children involved. This can affect the mental health and education of these children as resources become scarce. This isn't to say that it is not possible to have a healthy relationship, but there is a cost to the health of the relationship to child ratio, pending environmental and resource factors. We will speak more about fatherhood and sex in later chapters. I felt it was important to tie this point together as it relates to behavior and education.

Communal/Community

I grew up at a time when if you got in trouble at school, not only did your mother hear about it, but your neighbor, your bus driver, the store clerk, the local vagrant, and others all knew what you did by the time you came home. Your education and behavior in school were not limited to the school. In Secretary Clinton's book "It takes a village" she writes "The Village can no longer be defined as a place on a map, or a list of people or organizations, but its essence remains the same: it is the network of values and relationships that support and affect our lives" [112]

In this politically polarized day, I could not say with great confidence that the village or community can take on the issues of the day as it relates to the community need. School Boards were influential in neighborhood diversification and acceptance; School Boards approved reading materials; parents' rights; child safety and neighbor awareness; and other areas of community. In the news today, we hear about many of the changes that the school boards want to impose on teachers and how they teach. School boards were community first and national identity second. The national fervor changed the hearts of the school board members and led them to give preference to national identity. The Overton Window of education went from trust in educators and the administrators, those who have dedicated their lives to education, and become opinion and politics-based with little focus on the path forward for our children. The crisis facing the education of boys is biased by the political and opinion-based nature of our current society. The data shows that this is a critical crisis that will affect all young people as they move towards adulthood.

One of the more influential groups of people in a person's life are their teachers. Teachers help young people find their calling in life. Teachers take on the roles of parents, confidants, best friends, advisors, disciplinarians, standard bearers, and guardians to adulthood. The influence a teacher has on a child's life is second only to their parents and peers and can be the defining line between success and failure. If a teacher can influence a child at an early enough age, the child will have a better relationship with school and the subjects the influencing teacher teaches. Teaching had once been a male-dominated industry. Some of the greatest philosophical teachers were men. Teaching was also aligned with social and economic power. The first lessons learned were at home with mom or a caretaker (usually female). As cities grew, the need for primary education became a greater public interest, and the opportunity for women to become members of the working class presented itself. Women have been able to use teaching as a means to support their families, teaching helped Women's Rights through economic independence, professionalization, unionization and advocacy, and leadership roles.

Teaching, along with Nursing, are part of the few female-dominated industries. To this day, there continues to be a gap in the percentage of women in academia, which has typically been male-dominated. There are metadata analyses and studies that show changes to what was once considered the norm in academia. In the study "Exploring Gender Bias in Six Key Domains of Academic Science: An Adversarial Collaboration," the authors write "A recent analysis challenges the widespread assumption that sexism consistently disadvantages women in academic science. The authors found that, among tenure-track faculty, women and men perform equally across several key areas—grant funding, journal acceptance rates, and recommendation letters—and that women are slightly favored in hiring. However, the study also noted modest but real disparities in teaching evaluations and salaries, with women receiving lower ratings and slightly less pay. While these gaps were smaller than often reported, the authors emphasized that broader social and structural barriers may still limit women's advancement in academic fields."[113]

Supporting this, a 2014 meta-analysis encompassing over 1.6 million students (346 effect sizes across 227 studies) examined gender differences in academic performance and variability. The findings aligned with the long-discussed variability hypothesis: male grades tended to show greater spread than female grades, meaning boys were more often found at both the highest and lowest ends of achievement. Interestingly, the greatest variability difference appeared in non-STEM subjects, not in math or science as traditionally expected. On average, female students outperformed male students overall, confirming earlier research by Voyeur and Voyeur. The authors concluded that while gender differences in variability are small, they are consistent and influenced more by subject area than by age or grade level.[114]

I include this information to underline the importance of understanding the difference between our potential preconception of the realities of academia for both male and female professors and students, and the trending reality. We cannot make effective change based on biased or impartial information. We need to continue to evaluate and understand the current and trending circumstances to make effective forward progress. Equality is allowing both the same opportunity for success; however, we need equity to balance the scales to equality.

Teaching has problems with inequality and biases towards both male and female students. The bias towards students is in how teachers grade male and female students in math and sciences, as well as a bias towards boys in STEM classes. The present data show that girls do better in STEM classes, but there remains a bias in encouraging women to enter STEM professions. This has been a changing trend, with great efforts made by many individuals and programs, and the number of women in STEM has increased in the past few decades. Again, this is not to say that women have achieved a level playing field; it is to show an improvement in STEM jobs and to show how effective efforts to improve the ratio of women employed in these fields have been made during the push to get more women into STEM jobs. This is in contrast with the need to ensure that we also keep boys in mind when we look at the overall efforts made towards equalization.

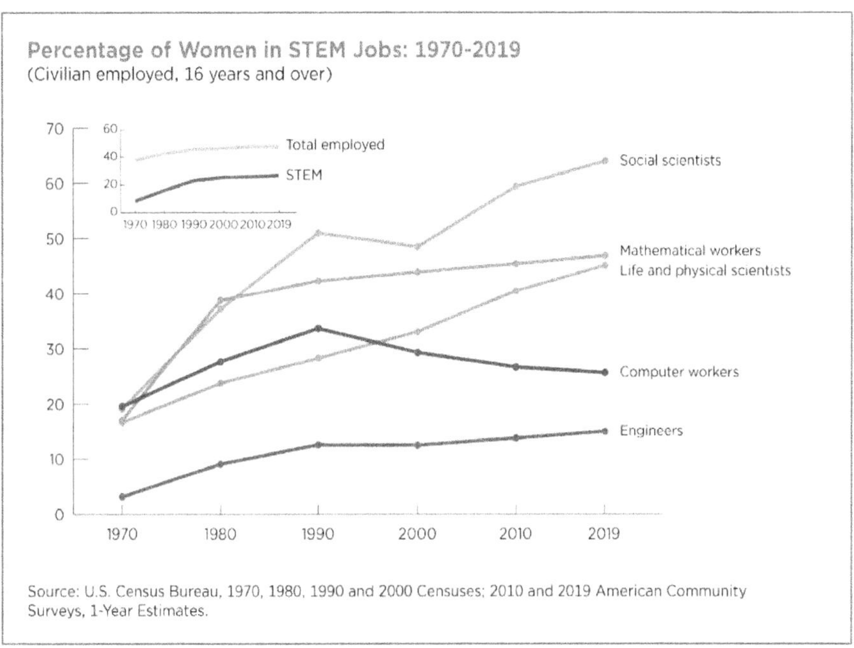

Source: U.S. Census Bureau, 1970, 1980, 1990 and 2000 Censuses; 2010 and 2019 American Community Surveys, 1-Year Estimates.

The other reality is that boys are underperforming in school in all classes. Even with the STEM bias, boys are not meeting the challenge of their educational requirements. Community solutions to help improve grades include:

Hiring More Male Teachers

- Promote hiring retired or end-of-career professionals to teach the next generation.
- *Promote Big Bother/Big Sister programs*

- Provide tax incentives, along with community buy-in in to help take the time to foster relationships with those that may not have strong positive male role models.

- *Alternative Teaching Solutions*
    - Adopting alternate teaching solutions for boys and girls that may not fit in a traditional school setting, i.e., data and results-driven teaching programs, remote learning, homeschooling, and other similar programs

- *Community Data and result focus*
    - Community efforts to improve and expand efforts to gain data around how effectively students learn, which teachers are the most effective, and review the most effective teaching systems, which would include community feedback and coordination.

- *Afterschool and Tutoring*
    - Funding for after-school programs that are subject-specific and provide incentives for community members to take charge of helping improve the quality and level of education.

- *Empathy*
    - I will speak more about empathy on a societal level later in the book. I want to note in this section the importance of including lessons that cover the Emotional Quotient spectrum. A focus on I.Q. and E.Q. will help all children, especially boys, to allow for the inclusion of their feelings and acceptance of these feelings. Too often, boys are told not to cry or show emotion. In providing direction on how to properly channel those feelings and emotions and work with

others through their emotions; boys will feel confident in how they engage the world, understanding that the stigma associated with qualities that are seen as "less masculine", are meaningless and do not provide care for their mental or physical health, only to lead to their death and destruction.

Many of these solutions come from the "It takes a village" model of child rearing. As with the need to improve the lives and welfare of girls and women, it is necessary to implement many of these efforts to help save our young boys as they grow to become men. I stress that these are ideas to start the discussion that will incorporate real world data, the entire village, as well as data analysis, as we look for the solutions. These solutions require metrics to measure effectiveness of understand where improvement is needed and a willingness to build change in the process.

Technological

In the realm of technology, education has always been one of the first sectors that benefits from new technological advancements, as it become commercialized. The ability of schools to bulk purchase educational software and materials helps ensure the availability and continued push for improvement. There is a lot of waste on new technology, at times, and the upper to middle income schools tend to receive the more advanced teaching technologies before schools in low income neighborhoods.

Capitalism and the quest for the almighty buck push for creativity, new concepts and fast-to-market publishing. This is where a community/government agency could help, both by providing additional data to the companies that create these technologies, while the community/government agencies design strategic outlines that give these companies guidelines on the overall teaching plan. These plans would create custom modules for various neighborhoods that will help bring equity to the areas of study that have students have historically had trouble with in low-income neighborhoods.

With low technology solutions, like using real-world examples of educational concepts, students can tour the Palace of Versailles while discussing French history, they can see how an engineer or carpenter uses geometry to help build a rocket ship or table while including students in the process, and they can watch videos of both cartoons and actual in-body videos of the immune system in action. Treat students like the "smaller adults" they are. The concept of hot does not become real to a child until they feel the heat and/or searing pain. This type of sensory learning could be used to help bring teaching concepts to life (I am not advocating for burning children).

Data and research-driven technologies are great ways to help improve the availability of various learning tools, but we must have community involvement with the creation and use of these tools, as well as mental health assessments. Teaching children how to check in on their mental health and having that awareness are critical to improving the devices and programs children use for self-improvement and self-care. It also provides a check-in mechanism to process their feelings - how the product makes them feel about the world, themselves, reality, and others. This will help monitor dissociative disorders or unintended consequences like addiction.

In closing, to improve the educational future of our boys and girls, we must ensure that any solutions to help boys are also used to help bolster and support other children and include the following:

- The community and government work hand in hand to find solutions that benefit the children in their communities. Data and information are the cornerstone of any solution or solution-based process. Ensuring that data points and users' information are stored and secured in a government facility where access requires the highest government clearance, and distribution is only provided on air gapped networks.

- Children have access to tools and supportive people, places or things that they can call upon to help them as they work through childhood. Continuous check-ins with children, as well as counseling opportunities, are important to gaining trust to help resolve issues that may prevent a child from reaching their full potential. Mental health challenges should be seen as opportunities to help a child reach their potential when used in conjunction with various mental health care options available. Ensuring that IQ and EQ are viewed as equally important in the eyes of the school systems, parents, the community, and society as a whole is equally important.

- Understanding that drugs may not always be the solution to behavioral challenges, however, as a solution, more information should be available to avoid the stigma of these support options. More rigorous testing, more science-based decision-making, more science-based education to parents, teachers and society as a whole.

- Society must be open to new and different solutions to problems that have not been solved through healing and supportive means. The community must be willing to be part of the solution and the eventual actions required for success. Teachers are an extension of the community and are the figureheads of the village that the community represents. An increase in the number of male teachers, male mentors, and addressing the inherent bias towards boys and girls is a must in improving the overall education system.

- Tough and honest conversations will be needed at school board meetings. There are many options presented in game theory that communities can use to find a resolution to contentious issues. Too many children are at risk due to the static nature of politics and our current bureaucratic systems. There are techniques used all around the world that can be implemented in schools to resolve these log jams. This also means holding both social and corporate media to a higher standard of information and content that works in the framework of these implemented solutions. We also have AI modeling that can be used to help provide options and potential results of different programs. Each school that changes how it teaches its students and addresses the problems that its students face can share this information on a local, national, and international level.

Fatherhood and Mentoring

I will start this chapter with the birth of Aurora Elizabeth Williams. Her name was almost Aurora Elizabeth Josephine Williams, to get as many letters in the alphabet into her name and to name her after one of our favorite TV characters from the show "Eureka." That was a hard no from her mother when naming time came. Many years ago, Aurora saved my life. I was going through a bout of depression caused by the sexual assault and bullying I was experiencing. I had decided one day to take some ibuprofen, one after another, after another. I fell asleep and nothing happened. I went to school the next day, and my nose started bleeding and did not stop. I told my teacher what happened, and the fire department and ambulance came to take me to the hospital. It was recommended that I see a counselor with my grandmother. I remember speaking with the counselor telling her she couldn't use mind tricks on me. I also remember my grandmother crying when I told her about my self-hate and loathing. I never told her about the sexual abuse.

After seeing my grandmother cry, I told myself that I would do better for her and I did not want to see her in pain again. I remember having a vision of a little girl about 8 or 9. She said to me, "Daddy, everything will be alright." I then asked her for her name, and she said, "My name is Aurora." I knew from that day that I would have a daughter and her name would be Aurora. I remember on my first date with her mother, we spoke about children, and I told her the story. She said she loved the name. When Aurora was born, we had agreed to play the song "The Road" by Zero 7 (which is playing right now as I type this; this synchronicity thing is really unnerving). When her head crowned, I became a father. All the preparation and classes led up to this moment. I can't say I fell in love with her when I laid eyes on her for the first time, because I was always in love with her. I had been in love with her since I was about 13/14. I stayed with her the entire time while they checked her out. I knew it was her crying even after they had taken her out of the room. This was the start of fatherhood for me, and even though her mother and I are no longer together, we have found ways to be a strong parenting team for our daughter.... much of it starts with my responsibilities as a father.

I did not grow up with my father. I intimately understand what a child misses when that father figure is not consistently in their lives. As I reflect on the recent passing of my uncle Manzie Jr, I think about one of my first memories of meeting him. My brother and I were visiting our grandparents' house in Ohio. He walked through the back door, and when I saw him, my eyes got big and heavy with tears, and my heart both ached and filled with longing. I hadn't seen my father in years, and I thought he was my father. Uncle Manzie saw my face and said, "Boy, I ain't your father." The memory of those feelings have never left me and drives me to be the father I am today. I am lucky to have had many male role models in my life. There is great truth to the impact a man can have on a child's life. My grandfather Manzie, Mr. Johnson, Mr. Brown, Pastor John, Deacon Harry are the first images of male figures that enter my mind when I think of those who were father figures to me as a young child.

The start of the recognition of a father's role begins in infancy. A child may not be able to observe all of the people around it, but it will recognize voices from out of the womb. Touch is also an important part of bonding with a child, which is why both mothers and fathers are encouraged to set aside time for skin-to-skin contact. In "Why Dads and Their Babies Need to Go Skin to Skin" the author Mary Steen ' writes about studies that have shown improved stress relief in fathers who provide "Kangaroo Care" to their babies. [115] As a baby begins to see, it then associates touch, audio and visual pairings with its parents or caretakers. As children grow, they begin to associate behaviors with gender. It starts like a matching list of random traits that get keyed from more grand concepts to specialized meanings. It's part of the reason why children want to touch and put things into their mouths. They are branching out their associative connections. This is the natural progress of our social nature. We are social beings. Many of the great apes, our evolutionary cousins, exhibit these traits. The larger question is whether or not our behavior is based on environmental factors or genetics. The scientific consensus is that both play a role.

There are a myriad of factors that play into genetics; there are master switches in utero that turn on and off various genetic traits. There are potential environmental factors that may cause one switch to be selected rather than another. We know that drugs, alcohol and tobacco affect children. We know that Lead can affect a child in utero and after birth. We know that mothers share their immunity with their children. With all of the genetic factors at play, we are limited in both our understanding and ability to safeguard against many genetic anomalies. Until the time when genetic therapeutics and gene editing using techniques like CRISPR are found to be safe and effective, the one area where we do have control is the environment children grow. The way a father behaves is an environmental factor that affects their child. Each interaction, each cuddle, scolding, caress, raised voice, hand hold, tickle fight, deep conversation, every tear seeps into the heart of the child. Children want to please their parents, and in time, they want to be their own person. The love of a father is a specialized love that comes only from a father.

Societal

The role of the father has stayed the same in society from hunter-gatherer to today. A father is the protector and breadwinner in the family. A father is the strong, dominant partner in the household. If art imitates life, the strongest examples of fatherhood come from TV shows, movies, and art. "Leave it to Beaver" and "Father Knows Best" were examples of the apex of a father's responsibilities. Shows like the "Andy Griffith Show", "Little House on the Prairie" were shows that gave fathers another dynamic where they were widowers who took on a softer and nurturing nature at times. You can't go full nurture, of course, because you would then feminize the fathers, rhetorically speaking of course. During the post-Civil Rights Era, the more prominent fathers at those times were mirrored images of the contrast in American culture - Mike Brady (The Brady Bunch) and James Evan Sr. (Good Times). These were two different types of fathers coming from two different worldviews. One was a man living in a medium to upper-income two-story household in the suburbs with a wife, six children and a maid. The other lived in a two-bedroom apartment in the Cabrini Green Housing project with a wife and four kids on the North Side of Chicago.

Mr. Brady was the smart, educated, well-mannered, doting father with the occasional word of wisdom spoken after his wife had already resolved the issue or if there was a need for the father's closing remarks. Mr. Evans was a street-wise, hardworking, stern and strict man, who was the last word in the house. Both fathers demanded more of their children; one father also had the luxury of allowing his children to fail, while the other did not. These are two examples of the contrast of fatherhood as portrayed as art imitating life. I grew up with three TV father figures – Alphonse Hercules Bundy, Dan Connor and Dr. Heathcliff Huxtable. These were the three most dominant male figures on TV during my childhood. Al Bundy was a man's man, and his gripes about society were the gripes of the common man, the everyday man. Al Bundy was the hyperbolic embodiment of what society thought men think about on a daily basis - Hot women, Cold Beer, and Football. Dan Conner was a more realistic portrayal of the everyday father, at least in rural America. He liked cold beers and football, but had eyes for one woman, his wife. Dan was soft, understanding, and a cuddly bear. He stood his ground with his wife and worked together to figure out the best solution for their family. Dan had that hidden physical strength that he rarely needed to display, but he was not afraid to use that power to protect his family. Dan had his demons, but he was able to push through to the other side to protect and secure his family. Dr. Huxtable was an educated, soft-spoken, kind-hearted, goofy, affable father who was supportive of his children in their education and growth. Dr. Huxtable was rarely the intimidating father figure. He used stories and his own life lessons to get his point across. He shared a deep physical and emotional connection with his children, providing a perfect balance to his wife's more executive and mature nature. We have had a myriad of these father archetypes in TV shows like "Modern Family", "My Wife and Kids", "Rules to date my Daughter", "Family Matters", "The Fresh Prince of Bel Air", and many more.

Boys are shown what society's ideal fathers should be like, and they then ask themselves, "Where is my father?" or "Why is my father not like this?" We do not tell boys, young men and fathers that these people are not reality. The reality is we can be more than what these fathers are by being more in the opportunities we have with our children. The important takeaway, from a societal standpoint, is that all of these fathers were there for their children through the good and the bad.

These fictional fathers provided support as needed and let their children find their way through the problem. *Dr. Farrell* writes about the difference between how a father teaches a child and how a mother teaches a child. A mother wants to protect their child from the world, which is a parental instinct. Both parents want to protect their child; however, men understand that society is not set up to help men, and therefore, men have to be able to do the heavy lifting and move forward when they need to. This is a lesson fathers also teach their daughters. Society is set up to provide safe havens for women and children. When a father teaches a child, they are teaching the child how to use their own abilities to survive in the world. This is the difference between how men see the world and how women see the world. [116] Men are expected to be Atlas and put the world on their shoulders. Atlas was a God; we are humans. Since society has evolved to see women as the weaker sex, women are afforded more vulnerability. We are all human. We need to learn how to push humanity forward together, and also learn how important self-care is.

Mothers and fathers provide a child with balance. Pushing the envelope to do better and be better, while affording ourselves self-care, love, and understanding, are part of how we build a contrasting balance for ourselves in child care. The weight of upholding society should not fall solely on men. Efforts are being made to spread these societal efforts among men and women. The efforts do not counteract the damage already done to men and women, respectively. The burden on men is taught to men by their fathers, father figures, and society through their beliefs and actions. When a father abandons his family, he is creating an undue burden on both the mother and child. Dr. Farrell goes into more detail on this. He writes about how children internalize abandonment. Children believe their parents' leaving is their fault. Dr. Farrell also writes that mothers need to take care in how they speak about the child's father to prevent further psychological damage. If a mother speaks poorly about the father on one hand, and says the child looks like or is like their parent, that can create associative trauma in the child. Society has to do more to provide fathers with positive images of fatherhood and manhood.[117] A great example that contributes to this is found in one of the great fathers of TV history, Homer Jay Simpson. In episode 1 of Season 1 of "The Simpsons," Lisa Simpson had the following exchange with her Aunt Patty:

"**Patty:** It's almost nine o'clock.

Selma: Where is Homer, anyway?

Patty: It's typical of the big doofus to spoil it all.

Lisa Simpson: What, Aunt Patty?

Patty: Oh, nothing, dear. I'm just trashing your father.

Lisa Simpson: Well, I wish that you wouldn't. Because aside from the fact that he has the same frailties as all human beings, he's the only father I have. Therefore, he is my model of manhood, and my estimation of him will govern the prospects of my adult relationships. So I hope you bear in mind that any knock at him is a knock at me, and I am far too young to defend myself against such onslaughts."[118]

Being a man is part of our collective humanity, and it should be celebrated the same as all other personhoods. There is great positivity in Women's History Month, Black History Month, Latin Heritage Month, and other such monthly observations. The message is to show and honor the great contributions that these underrepresented communities have provided to humanity. Fathers and men have also contributed to society and humanity. We should celebrate men who are the archetypes for the society we want to evolve into. The names may change over time as the Overton Window changes, but the impact that these types of men have on the image and definition of what a man or a father are is priceless. If our society admires and needs more men like Mr. Rogers, a man beyond reproach, then this image of masculinity should be appreciated the same in men and by society. Mr. Rogers was a great man, a great father, a great teacher and a great human.

How men see themselves vs how they see other men

In a research article in the "Journal for Men's Studies," the author's found that men have a greater opinion of masculinity when they compare the masculinity of other men. The abstract reads as follows "….The present research examines men's perceptions of how traditional masculinity norms are viewed by three reference groups: society as a whole, other men, and women. We assessed these perceptions via two experiments based on the self-presentation paradigm and involving American

(N=161) or British (N=160) men. Participants in both experiments perceived traditional masculinity as being valued by other men but not by society as a whole or by women … Across two experiments in the United States and the United Kingdom, they found that men believed *other men* valued traditional masculinity far more than either women or society at large. Interestingly, each man's own level of identification with these norms closely aligned with what he thought other men valued, suggesting that men's self-concepts are strongly shaped by their assumptions about peer expectations rather than broader cultural approval."[119]

In the Pew Research report "How Americans See Men and Masculinity" surveyors were asked a series of questions that asked whether or not certain traits were manly or masculine and whether or not there was too little or too much value of these traits in society. There were some interesting results shown in the study. As part of the study there was also a delineation between Republican/Conservative viewpoints and Democrat/Liberal viewpoints. In an earlier discussion we talked about the link between masculinity and how audience view more liberal leaning actors vs conservative actors in action movies and their caliber of action stardom. In the study they found that 43% of all adults believe that people in the US have positive views of men who are manly or masculine, while 25% have negative views, the remaining have neither positive nor negative viewpoints. Of that breakdown 36% of men have a positive views of men who are manly or masculine, while 33% had negative views. Within these numbers 45% of the Republican leaning responders believe that people in the US have negative views while 20% of democratic leaning men believe people in the US have a negative view. [120] There are further breakdowns in the study and I implore readers review the survey. It is very easy to follow and provides additional context and explanation. My take away from reading this survey shows that there is a realignment already happening as it relates to the view of what masculinity is and can be. The purpose of this book is to help with the societal push towards helping redefine what masculinity is so that men can save themselves and future generations from the yoke of masculinity that causes an intergeneration trauma to our society and our boys.

The Goodness of Man

The Book of Romans, a book in the Christian bible, has influenced my life in the writings of Paul. In Romans chapter 3, he writes about the goodness of man.

Romans 3:23 - "For all have sinned and fall short of the glory of God."

At times when I read this I think of, "God" as society. Men have sinned and failed in the eyes of society. Some men have made great contributions towards the benefit of humanity, and sadly, in society, their transgressions outshine their contributions. It is important to separate fatherhood and manhood and allow for restorative justice in both areas of a man's life. Humanity is not one person or one action. Humanity is a system where beliefs and actions are part of the whole. The individual and the whole require reflection from the viewpoint at the pinnacle of what humanity can be.

The lens of history will change, humanity will change, and we are the sum of all that comes before. We are participants in the timeline of humanity and work towards the realization of those dreams. In order to benefit from each individual, our society must be willing to allow for restorative justice and separate the dichotomy of good and evil. Sin has to be dealt with through the process of restorative justice, and the good is honored for its impact. Those two processes cannot be separated. As the sun brings more details to light, the shadows entreat reality. A father sees himself as the sum of who he is and all that he has done. As a man, he may not believe that he is capable of being greater than the worst parts of his life. Society's responsibility is to ensure that all people can contribute their best selves towards the course of advancing humanity. We all lose when fathers feel lost and incapable of giving the best of themselves to their children and to humanity. The goal is never to shame. The goal is always to allow for a path forward. Growth is to be recognized and acknowledged, and at the same time challenged and held responsible.

In fatherhood, both the father and the child grow and mature together. Many of us who grew up while our parents were in their teens or twenties may not realize, until later in life, that our parents were also children. Fathers are products of masculinity, and masculinity is a product of society. Society and children need fathers to be active participants in the lives of their children. All fathers want the love and respect of their children. To have respect, men must be and do better, as both humans and as fathers, when the opportunity arises. Society must do better in how masculinity, manhood, and the male identity are treated. Restorative justice is not a one-way street. The victim is compensated, and the perpetrator can find redemption. When society elevates redemption and compensation to the same level, only then can we heal.

Creating Fatherhood programs in communities can have an immediate and direct impact on fathers and families. Some examples of these types of programs are:

The National Responsible Fatherhood Clearing House (NRFC):

The US government website "The National Responsible Fatherhood Clearing House," which is a part of the U.S. Department of Health and Human Services. Their mission statement is "The goals of the National Responsible Fatherhood Clearinghouse (NRFC) are to provide, facilitate, and disseminate current research and proven and innovative strategies that will encourage and strengthen fathers and families and providers of services via the following activities:

- Robust NRFC website – *www.Fatherhood.gov*

- *Media Campaign* that promotes the Responsible Fatherhood field and efforts of local programs

- Social media engagement via X, *Facebook*, *Instagram*, *YouTube*, and *LinkedIn*

- Development and dissemination of *written products* that advance responsible fatherhood research and practice

- Outreach and presentations at *conferences and events*

- National Call Center for dads and practitioners (1-877-4DAD411)

- *Virtual trainings*

- A *Virtual Collaborative Community (VCC)* for Fatherhood Stakeholders

There is also documentary about fatherhood, dad jokes, mental health information and links to various other resources to help with fatherhood. [121]

Global Fatherhood Foundation

Their vision is "To transform communities by inspiring fathers to help their children be the best they can be. We advocate for co-engaging our communities and support a vision that all communities and human service organizations are proactively father-inclusive so that every child has an involved, responsible, and committed father."[122]

Men Care - A Global Fatherhood Campaign

MenCare is a global fatherhood campaign active in more than 60 countries on five continents, coordinated by Equimundo: Center for Masculinities and Social Justice (formerly Promundo-US) and Sonke Gender Justice. Our mission is to promote men's involvement as equitable, nonviolent fathers and caregivers in order to achieve family well-being, gender equality, and better health for mothers, fathers, and children. We aim for men to be allies in supporting women's social and economic equality, in part by taking on more responsibility for childcare and domestic work. We believe that true equality will only be reached when men take on 50 percent of the world's child care and domestic work.[123]

Black Men Build – ""We are Black Men working with Black Men to serve our communities, to be critical freethinkers, to speak truth, to teach others, and to build the social, economic, political, and spiritual tools needed to evolve and power Black futures.

Other initiatives are *"The Fatherhood Charter,"*[124] which outlines that the Global Fatherhood Charter was drafted in consultation with 21 leading child development researchers across the world in 2019, to help clarify the issues for all those supporting fatherhood in child development across the world: parents, practitioners and policy makers. It draws on the conclusions of a large body of research.

This is the charter as found on their website

https://childandfamilyblog.com/global-fatherhood-charter/

1. The loving care of a father is a foundation for his child's well-being and creates a lifelong relationship.

2. The loving care of a father can be as powerful and important as that of a mother.

3. All fathers, both biological and non-biological, have an innate ability to bond with their babies from the first days. A father's brain changes when he actively cares for his child, generating enhanced capacity for care and empathy.

4. Loving care takes many forms. Each family and each father-child relationship is unique.

5. Fathers are family, and family carers are among the most important influences on children's development, wellbeing and health. This is so even when fathers do not live permanently with their children.

6. A harmonious community of care around a child, with parents and carers supporting each other, is a foundation for the child's healthy development.

7. Fatherhood, like motherhood, is a journey. Fathers need time and practice to care for, nurture, play with, and teach their children.

8. Loving fatherhood means respect for and collaboration with the mother and the absence of violence.

9. To provide the care and form the relationships that children need, fathers need support and validation from their partners, families, communities and society.

10. Maternal and newborn health services, early years services, and economic self-sufficiency services should offer and encourage the use of, support for fathers and other family carers in ways that engage creatively with the local culture and socioeconomic conditions. They should provide information and help about how to support maternal and child health and child development. They should support family carers' relationships with their children and a harmonious community of care for children within families. They should offer support for all carers to meet their children's financial needs. This support should be accessible to fathers even if they live apart from the mother.

11. Workplaces and employment laws should honour and support the caring responsibilities of both fathers and mothers.

12. Fathers' involvement in the first 1,000 days of their children's lives should be a focus of international early childhood development strategies.

13. Promotion of gender equality needs to include support for fatherhood. Equal economic opportunities for women and men must include the opportunity to share the care of their children.

14. Men are inherently loving and caring beings. Men's caring instincts and emotional life should be celebrated as part of what it is to be a man in today's cultures.

15. Loving fatherhood and men's caregiving of all kinds should be recognised and celebrated as an inspiration to other fathers, mothers, grandparents and carers, in this generation and the next."[125]

There are also various media outlets that have built social networks to help empower fathers and father figures. *"The Dad Edge Live Legendary"* by Larry Hagner is a Podcast that focuses on "parenting, mindset, patience, communication, intimacy, optimizing health, and the power of community," through interviews and resources." [126] Dr. Warren Farrel was a guest on their podcast.

Child Support and the uplifting of fathers

The child support system is a social system that was created to help custodial parents continue to provide for their children to a level that would be close to or on par with the shared resources the collective family unit would have provided. I will speak more about the concept of marriage and dating in a future section, but at this time, I will discuss the initial genesis of this situation - sex. Dr. Farrell notes that men need to be more protective of themselves and their genetics.[127] Society has this image of men as base creatures controlled by our sexual urges and desires. This minimizes what a man is and the care and love required by him. Society, as a product of humanity, has a responsibility to allow people to be vulnerable, open, and honest about their feelings. Society has a responsibility to help men be more responsible with their reproductive abilities, the same as the rights women have/had, depending on what state you live in. When the US government saw drugs as the scourge of the nation, it created the D.A.R.E. program to counter the rise in drug use. The government went after "Big Pharma" for the Opioid pandemic. The government has had a hand in education reform, race/sex discrimination reform, economic reform, and many other changes to society. We need more discussions and social change related to sex, sexual education, and fatherhood. We are in a time when schools are pushing to remove sex education from schools.

During the 90's, when the teen birth rate was accelerating, schools used sex education as a means to help limit teen pregnancies. There is no male birth control pill at the time of this writing, yet there is a pill to promote male sex drive. This continues to perpetuate the narrative that men are only their penises. Is it socially responsible to have children at ages that will not allow the father and child the opportunities to bond, learn, and teach each other? Or the reverse, where we have children having children, where the adult brain does not mature until the age of 25/26? As a society, we need to have a serious dialogue about sex and sexual education, including the mental and physical risks to the child associated with having children at the extreme ends of life.

The child support system is not a product of a child's birth. It is a product of the patriarchal system in America as well as the masculine identity. The courts, as well as society, recognize mothers as the better caretakers. The 2017 Census shows the percentage of custodial mothers receiving child support averaged about 55% from 1999 to 2001 and from 2003 to 2017, to 56% an increase of 1%. The number of custodial fathers receiving child support averaged about 40% from 2003 to 2017; the number reduced to 36%. This same data shows us that custodial fathers had full-time jobs at a rate of about 70% and for women, it was lower, but the part-time job difference between men and women was much greater, where it could be deduced that most of these mothers had two or more part-time jobs. The number of women working full-time steadily increased. The numbers show that though more men are becoming custodial parents, the percentage of child support received must increase on both ends. Men need to provide child support in both a monetary, social and physical sense, and women also need to pay their share of child support as well.[128] Men will suffer in silence, which will ultimately affect their children. Even on the other end, where fathers pay child support, men will also suffer in debt working to pay child support. When men are in arrears, there is evidence showing increases in alcohol abuse and depression.[129]

It is important that men, as well as women, seek ways to better enforce child support. With that said, the system also needs to overhaul how it determines the monthly support payments. Payment systems factor in the time spent with the child/children, salary, living expenses, average needs of a child based on educational needs, age, location, and other factors; all while ensuring that the child's physical and mental health is taken care of, all based on the salary of both parents. Dr. Farrell also recommends including parent coordinators to help deal with difficult situations that may come up during co-parenting. This should also be accounted for in the numbers, as well as family and child therapy. [130]

Fatherhood is an essential part of the fabric of our society and does not receive the same risk assessment as poverty, drugs, alcohol, gangs, mental health, and many other factors that can put a child at risk of becoming a victim of society's failings. As a society, we should uplift fathers to true greatness and provide services that will help fathers reach their full potentials. Child rearing is not done alone or in isolation. Parents must also learn to communicate and learn the fundamentals of child development. Parent kits, similar to those provided in Scandinavian countries, should become the standard, not the outliers. There are resources available to fathers that they may not be aware of, and all efforts must be made to get this information into their hands. Every effort must be made to educate fathers and society on the importance of fathers and their role in the family. Society also has to do better in finding ways to improve the legal system as it relates to parental custody and the child support system.

Behavioral

The most important part of any interaction is empathy. As parents, we need to find ways to connect and be empathetic with our children. There is an abundance of literature that teaches how to build an empathetic relationship with a child. A quick internet search along with conversations with a counselor or therapist can help you outline the best ways to be empathetic. You have to find your own way to empathy, through interactions with your partner, your boss, your friends, your family and your children. There is no silver bullet or easy solution. Patience, as well as open and honest dialogue, along with self-awareness and humility, are the paths forward.

You may not get it right the first few times; no one ever does, but that is part of the process of getting better. You are building a bond, and it pays off over time (there's a finance joke in there somewhere). I told Aurora from the beginning of our relationship that I would never lie to her. I told her that there may be things that I may not be able to explain to her immediately, but I would tell her that. If I don't know the answer to a question, we search together. If she needs to talk, all distractions are put away, and she has my undivided attention. I challenge her thinking at times because I don't want her to parrot someone else's response. I want her to be able to show her math or the logic of her thinking. I will ask her *"How did you come to this conclusion?" "Did you consider these things?" "How can I better help you at this moment?"*

As fathers, we need to set the example of how we want our sons and daughters to be treated. All genders are capable of reaching a point of success in society. The path may be more difficult for one than the other, yet the opportunity exists, and we must teach our children not only to work towards those opportunities but also to be the catalyst for those opportunities, while paving a way for equity and equality. If you have the opportunity to right a wrong or set an example, you should take it, whether the child is there or not. The story in itself can be impactful. No child is alike, yet each deserves to become their true selves. They can do so within the cocoon of our parentage. This behavior also extends to our partners. We should set the example of how we want our children to receive and accept love from their partners. We can be that example in our relationships. Every kiss, hug, walk, date night, and every encounter can be a teachable moment.

Define and redefine value.

Fatherhood changes our relationship with children and how we see the world. The value of a dollar is never the same after having children. The change in value of fatherhood is critical to how men move the needle forward. The value of a smile, a handshake, and a dollar are the most valuable lessons fathers can teach. Teach through your experience what a smile has done for you. Explain how a smile can disarm and start a fight depending on who you use it on. Many have been slain, and many saved due to a smile. Explain how a man's smile and a woman's smile differ, and how to be a force for change using your smile. The greater value is in one's self-confidence and self-image. Teaching our children to love themselves and understand who they are is one of the greatest gifts we can leave behind. The gift becomes harder to leave behind when you are competing with the facades of time. This is when empathy and trust help carry the conversation. Self-love cannot be forced; it developed in oneself over time, with learning and patience. All too often, limitations of "vision" limit our understanding of the "other."

When we explain the significance of a handshake we show how the value of respect can transcend conversation and be conveyed through a simple, cohesive meeting of hands. I once had an after-hours, night-long conversation with a guy at a bar in NY about handshakes. We were talking briefly and shook hands. We both gave props to the other's handshake grip. We then spent hours talking about the different types of handshakes we've received over the years and how important a hand shake can be. Those moments caused momentary bonds that were built because of the shared experience of passed down masculinity.

In reflecting on that night, I realized that the conversation about the handshake also revolved around the different manners you are taught as a man, how we found that the "trust" in a handshake and the "man code" had fallen out of favor in society; your word was your bond. The more important part of that conversation was the loss of trust in manhood and the value of the handshake and what came with it. In the movie "Ocean's Eleven," the character Danny Ocean used the "shaking of Frank Sinatra's hand" as a plot device to introduce the bond of manhood between the characters. As fathers, we need to reinforce the teaching and value of trust in one's word and the importance of doing one's best. In the Bhagavad Gita, there is a passage, "O' Dhananjaya, fix your mind on duty, without any thought of the resulting success or failure, and achieve the steadiness of yoga." The value in the trust of one's word is also the understanding of what it means to be human. That is the greatest and most valuable piece of the conversation. Teaching our children the value of being a human and how we preserve and advance humanity through our intention. Our ability to love, trust, support, agree, disagree, respect and transcend, as needed, all move towards success – success for ourselves, our world, and humanity.

The last of these values to teach and discuss is finance, or the value of value. I did not grow up with a strong understanding of financial responsibility. I learned a great deal of what I know from people I have met working in the banking industry. I learned about books like "The Book That Beats the Market", "Rich Dad, Poor Dad", "Financial Planning for Dummies" and podcasts like, "The Alan Turner Show", "Money For the Rest of Us", even NPR's "Planet Money.". I did take home economics in junior high school, where I learned how to balance a checkbook. There are some men born into families that are great at balancing their checkbooks. Some men grow up knowing the 50/30/20 rule (50% of earnings go to your needs, 30% to savings, 20% to wants and desires). Society, as a whole, needs to do more to educate people about financial planning. As a father, we can set the example for value appreciation.

We can share the appreciation of a Porsche 911 or Lamborghini, and teach the value of the hard work and financing required to purchase these cars. We can teach the value of hard work and how it translates into our paychecks, the food on our tables, the house we live in, the rainy day and emergency funds we save, and our future retirement. Teach children the value of being prepared and ready, teach them about life insurance, life savings, how interest and credit can greatly impact their livelihoods, teach them about the value of exercise, mental health care, self-care and self-protection. Leave no stone unturned, especially when it comes to preparing our children for the world to come.

The final behaviors that fathers should adopt and implement are love, openness, and critical thinking. These three critical key areas are a multiplier for the other topics. Showing love and emotion and teaching our children, and each other, that it is ok to show emotion.

Men do cry. Men can complement other men. When our children are frustrated, they either lash out or cry. They are human just like us. We tend to forget that at times and let societal pressures dictate how we should be as men, when we are humans first. As a father, hiding your emotions only teaches your children to hide theirs. It is difficult to help them if they hide the difficulties they are facing. Our emotions, as well as all that we do with our children, should be done in love. Let them know every day that they are loved and you are there for them. There should be no doubt in a child's mind that their father loves them and that they can go to their father for any of their needs, or any respected and trusted adult for that matter. Always be curious and open to receiving feedback. Feedback from others, as well as your children. Openness requires humility and the ability to forgive. Forgiveness is not to forget but to understand that we are human, fallible and require love and understanding. We must learn to forgive: both to forgive others and to forgive ourselves.

As we do this, we become better as we move forward. Humility requires acknowledging that we do not know everything and are willing to learn from others. Be willing to step from behind the armor and take the love shown and given by others; be energized by it. Cultivate it and make it grow and mature. Be willing to learn and teach critical thinking skills to help your children survive the world and to understand the value of making choices when you are not there. Sit with your child and work on critical thinking together. The world is becoming more and more inundated with information, and it becomes more difficult for parents to monitor the information their children take in and verify the information they receive. In teaching critical thinking, we give our children a guide to seek the truth and to teach them that seeking the truth is not easy; there is hard work involved in finding the truth. The truth is never easy to find, but once you have it, you gain as a person and can contribute more to your overall understanding and knowledge.

As fathers, we cannot control the outside world; we can only control how we allow it to influence ourselves and our children. In order to make our children better, we have to work on becoming better. We have to remember that we are human beings and have hopes and dreams for ourselves and our children. Fatherhood is a gift that allows us to pass on our genetic materials, but also to continue our brief story in the epoch of humanity. In understanding our behavior and improving ourselves, we also ensure that we are improving our children and the next generations that follow. The goal is to be the stalwart and eliminate generational trauma while developing new behaviors that our children will use to be purposeful humans and pass on those better traits of humanity.

Before closing this section, I will add some related areas of interest that we should consider as fathers and as a society:

- ***Offering Paternity leave*** - This should be at a level similar to or better than what men are afforded in Scandinavian countries. Men should receive a minimum of 6 months off for paternity leave. Raising a child is not easy, and with the "live to work" mentality many companies have, the focus of the family gets lost when it should always be one of the main focuses in humanity.

- ***Quality Time*** - This has been explored a bit during the course of this chapter; however, I believe it is important to call this out again. Quality Time with your children is one of the best benefits of being a father. You get to see closely how they grow and mature over time. You get to see yourself in your children, both the good and the bad. Aurora's mother says Aurora and I are very similar, and we are. We raise her to be a critical thinker, and sometimes, when we have "discussions," she will paint me into a corner using logic, and I acknowledge and applaud her efforts. I owe her 50 dollars and now know that trees are plants.

- ***Mentorship*** - We touched on this subject as it pertains to fathers, but this is a matter that extends beyond fatherhood. In order for us to help improve the lives of other men, we have to start before they become men. There are hundreds of mentorship programs around the country whose goals are to provide mental health counseling, emotional, and educational support for young men around the world. Society needs to do more to help incentivize joining mentoring programs. It is not enough to use goodwill in a society where everything is transactional. Offering incentives is the best way to get more men involved in mentorship programs. The value of a child in the lens of our society's future is priceless.

Mental Healthcare

"Maybe that was part of the insult in Allen's comment, too. Maybe he hadn't just meant to say that I was cool, but also that he felt closer to me in some way than he did to Bob. Their friendship had sure boundaries of touch, affection and expression, and as a woman, I could break through those blocks as quickly and effortlessly as I had changed my sex. Those were the rules, it seemed. As a guy, you didn't make yourself vulnerable, and you didn't burden yourself or your buds with your doubt and fear. They didn't want to hear about it, and you didn't want to reveal it. But with a woman, it was easier immediately. You could speak freely and get away with it, or at least as freely as your customary reticence would allow." - From Self-Made Man: One Woman's year disguised as a man by Norah Vincent in the scene after informing her male bowling friends that "he" was in fact a "she" and explaining her project to them. [131]

Men and mental health can seem to be interchangeable terms when discussing gun violence in America. Everywhere the discussion about gun violence is raised, mental health is right behind. Mental health issues are not an issue from today's headlines; this has been an ongoing problem since the dawn of human history. Humans have always had to deal with the effects of genetic and/or physical differences in the neuropathy and its function. Prior to discussing men and mental health, let's discuss the history of mental illness, mental health care around the world and how the current state of mental health in America came to be.

Mental health disorders, in the time before antiquity, were seen as either spiritual afflictions or acts of the divine. In "History of Mental Illness" by Ingrid G. Farreras, she writes, "Throughout history, there have been three general theories of the etiology of mental illness: supernatural, somatogenic, and psychogenic. Supernatural theories attribute mental illness to possession by evil or demonic spirits, displeasure of gods, eclipses, planetary gravitation, curses, and sin. Somatogenic theories identify disturbances in physical functioning resulting from either illness, genetic inheritance, or brain damage or imbalance. Psychogenic theories focus on traumatic or stressful experiences, maladaptive learned associations and cognitions, or distorted perceptions."[132]

As we move from antiquity, the tragic misunderstanding of mental illness continued. "For millennia, society did not treat persons suffering from depression, autism, schizophrenia and other mental illnesses much better than slaves or criminals: they were imprisoned, tortured or killed. [133]

During the Middle Ages, mental illness was regarded as a punishment from God: sufferers were thought to be possessed by the devil and were burned at the stake, or thrown in penitentiaries and madhouses where they were chained to the walls or their beds. During the Enlightenment, the mentally ill were finally freed from their chains and institutions were established to help sufferers of mental illness."[134] The path towards understanding the body's role in these afflictions began with Hippocrates in 400 BC. "It was around 400 BC that Hippocrates (460–370 BC) attempted to separate superstition and religion from medicine by systematizing the belief that a deficiency in or especially an excess of one of the four essential bodily fluids (i.e., humors)—blood, yellow bile, black bile, and phlegm—was responsible for physical and mental illness. For example, someone who was too temperamental suffered from too much blood and thus, blood-letting would be the necessary treatment.

Hippocrates classified mental illness into one of four categories—epilepsy, mania, melancholia, and brain fever—and like other prominent physicians and philosophers of his time, he did not believe mental illness was shameful or that mentally ill individuals should be held accountable for their behavior." [135] Witches were women who may have suffered from mental illness and, at times, were burned at the stake. There are many contributors to what we understand about Mental Illness.

The shoulders that have paved the way forward:

- **Galen (AD 130–201)** – Expanded on Hippocrates' humoral theory, emphasizing the connection between physical health and temperament. Introduced early ideas of the brain as the center of thought and emotion.

- **Vincenzo Chiarugi (1759–1820)** – Implemented humane treatment for the mentally ill in Florence; advocated for moral and medical approaches instead of punishment and confinement.

- **Philippe Pinel (1745–1826)** – Known for "unchaining the insane" in Paris; pioneered moral treatment emphasizing compassion, structure, and dignity in psychiatric care.

- **Jean-Baptiste Pussin (1746–1811)** – Worked alongside Pinel, first introducing non-restraint methods and humane treatment within asylums.

- **William Tuke (1732–1822)** – Founded the York Retreat in England, promoting moral therapy based on kindness, respect, and purposeful activity for patients.

- **Benjamin Rush (1745–1813)** – Often called the "Father of American Psychiatry"; advocated for humane treatment and authored the first American textbook on mental diseases.

- **Dorothea Dix (1802–1887)** – Social reformer who campaigned for the establishment of state mental hospitals and improved living conditions for the mentally ill in the United States.

- **Franz Anton Mesmer (1734–1815)** – Proposed "animal magnetism" (mesmerism) as a healing force; laid groundwork for hypnosis and later psychological exploration of suggestion and the unconscious.

- **James Braid (1795–1860)** – Coined the term *hypnotism* and reframed mesmerism as a psychological, not mystical, phenomenon—opening doors to scientific study of the mind.

- **Jean-Martin Charcot (1825–1893)** – Used hypnosis to study hysteria and neurological disorders; his work deeply influenced Freud's understanding of the unconscious and psychosomatic illness.

- **Ambroise-Auguste Liébeault (1823–1904)** – Early practitioner of therapeutic hypnosis in Nancy; emphasized suggestion as a means of psychological healing.

- **Hippolyte Bernheim (1840–1919)** – Expanded Liébeault's work, demonstrating that suggestion could influence both physical and psychological states, further shaping early psychotherapy concepts.

- **Emil Kraepelin (1856–1926)** – Developed the first systematic classification of mental disorders based on symptoms and course, distinguishing between psychotic disorders such as dementia praecox (schizophrenia) and manic-depressive illness.

Standing on These Shoulders

- **Josef Breuer (1842–1925)** – Applied therapeutic talking methods in treating hysteria, notably with patient Anna O., revealing that expression of repressed emotions could relieve symptoms.

- **Sigmund Freud (1856–1939)** – Expanded Breuer's "talking cure" into psychoanalysis, formalizing the concepts of the unconscious, repression, and dream interpretation—integrating centuries of evolving thought into a cohesive psychological theory.[136]

Before discussing Psychoanalysis, let's discuss the Diagnostic and Statistical Manual of Mental Disorders or DSM, which was first published in 1813. "The DSM has undergone various revisions (in 1968, 1980, 1987, 1994, 2000, 2013), and it is the 1980 DSM-III version that began a multiaxial classification system that took into account the entire individual rather than just the specific problem behavior. Axes I and II contain the clinical diagnoses, including intellectual disability and personality disorders. Axes III and IV list any relevant medical conditions or psychosocial or environmental stressors, respectively. Axis V provides a global assessment of the individual's level of functioning. The most recent version -- the DSM-5-- has combined the first three axes and removed the last two. These revisions reflect an attempt to help clinicians streamline diagnosis and work better with other diagnostic systems, such as health diagnoses outlined by the World Health Organization."[137]

I would like the reader to note that Homosexuality was once listed in the DSM and has been removed from the DSM. This is an example of how science evolves with our understanding of human physiology, psychology, and humanity. The most recent version of the DSM is the DSM-5-TR. "DSM-5-TR is a text revision of DSM-5 and includes fully revised text and new references, clarifications to diagnostic criteria, and updates to ICD-10-CM codes since DSM-5 was published in 2013. It features a new disorder, prolonged grief disorder, as well as codes for suicidal behavior. It was developed with the help of more than 200 subject matter experts, and text updates are based on current scientific literature."[138]

Why is the DSM important? The American Psychiatric Association writes, "The Diagnostic and Statistical Manual of Mental Disorders (DSM) is the handbook used by healthcare professionals in the United States and much of the world as the authoritative guide to the diagnosis of mental disorders. DSM contains descriptions, symptoms and other criteria for diagnosing mental disorders. It provides a common language for clinicians to communicate about their patients and establishes consistent and reliable diagnoses that can be used in research on mental disorders. It also provides a common language for researchers to study the criteria for potential future revisions and to aid in the development of medications and other interventions."[139]

With our brief review and new found understanding of the history of mental health, we can move forward into Psychoanalysis and modern-day therapy. Psychoanalysis is defined "as a system of psychological theory and therapy that aims to treat mental conditions by investigating the interaction of conscious and unconscious elements in the mind and bringing repressed fears and conflicts into the conscious mind by techniques such as dream interpretation and free association."[140] From this was born Psychodynamic Therapy. The other therapy types are Behavioral, Cognitive Behavioral Therapy, and Humanistic Therapy. They are identified as follows:

Psychodynamic Therapy

Rooted in psychoanalytic theory, this form of therapy explores how unconscious patterns, early experiences, and unresolved conflicts influence present emotions and behavior. Sessions typically encourage open discussion to identify recurring thoughts or behaviors that may "contribute to psychological distress."

Behavioral Therapy

This approach is structured and action-oriented. It is based on the idea that behaviors are learned through experience and that maladaptive behaviors can be modified through specific interventions. The focus is on changing observable behavior rather than exploring unconscious processes.

Cognitive Behavioral Therapy (CBT)

CBT combines elements of cognitive and behavioral psychology. It operates on the principle that distorted thinking patterns can contribute to emotional difficulties and maladaptive behaviors. Treatment focuses on identifying and reframing unhelpful thoughts while developing healthier behavioral responses.

Humanistic Therapy

This perspective emphasizes individual self-awareness and personal growth. It assumes that people are the best authorities on their own experiences and aims to foster self-acceptance and authentic decision-making. Therapists provide empathy and support rather than interpretation or direction.[141]

We now have the history, the current standard for diagnosing mental illness, and the current methods of treatment for mental illness…. So why do we still have societal problems with mental illness? At one point in history, our nation was littered with mental health institutions. Growing up in Brooklyn, we would joke that you were either admitted to the G building at Kings County Hospital or Bellevue Hospital if you were thought to be mentally unhinged (*There's an Arkham Asylum joke in here somewhere*).

So how did our country build up its mental health care facilities, and what was the catalyst for their decline in America?

"In 1946, the federal government entered mental health policy with the passage of the National Mental Health Act. In 1949, it established the National Institute of Mental Health (NIMH). With both, the government promoted visions of progress and community in mental health care—a stark contrast to stagnant connotations of state hospital institutionalization. By the 1960s, in terms of policies from the environment to education, the public largely believed in the federal government's ability to meet society's needs. In this political context, the Joint Commission on Mental Illness and Health, a federal organization charged with surveying the resources and diagnostic and treatment methods for mental illness, published its findings as Action for Mental Health. This document detailed inadequacies in national mental health services and called for improvements in both state mental hospitals and community mental health care. In 1963, Congress then passed and President Kennedy signed the Community Mental Health Act of 1963 (CMHA. With the CMHA, Kennedy and Congress sought to decrease the number of institutionalized individuals by establishing self-sufficient and local mental health care centers.

Kennedy's personal motivations illustrate the federal idealism in community mental health care. With his New Frontier platform, Kennedy sought improvements in the nation's mental and physical health. He also aimed to unburden society of chronically dependent persons. In particular, he hoped to liberate the population of confined mentally ill patients through advancements in psychopharmacology and supportive housing. He was emotionally drawn to issues of mental illness and intellectual disability because of his sister Rosemary, who underwent a lobotomy that significantly worsened her quality of life. Politically, Kennedy grasped the negative public sentiment around an increasing institutionalized population and its associated cost to the states. Kennedy's special message to Congress on February 6, 1963, captured his sense of optimism as he promoted a plan to "Cut by half, within a decade or two, the 600,000 persons now institutionalized for psychological disorders."

An overwhelmingly Democratic Congress (Senate 65% and House 59%) aligned with Kennedy on political and ideological sentiments. The Senate and House of Representatives introduced identical bills that outlined the terms of temporary federal financial support for the initial construction and staffing of community mental health centers. Despite financial concerns, illustrated by a Bureau of Budget internal memo that read, "The real question is who is going to finance operating costs once the federal subsidies are ended or indeed if they can be ended," bipartisan belief existed within both chambers that the CMHA's vision was a more hopeful and humanistic alternative to institutional care. This belief was rooted in a deep trust in medicine's promise to eliminate illness. Congressional members generally lacked medical knowledge, and many accepted claims about community mental health centers without probing. As preeminent mental health historian Gerald Grob wrote, a "euphoric atmosphere" existed within Congress surrounding the possibilities of community mental health care. In the end, the Senate (72-1) and House (335-18) wholly approved the CMHA." [142]

I used the entirety of this article because it truly captures the essence of the history of Mental Health Care Reform. From what we have read, mental health care became a state and community-coordinated social program. The laws passed in 1944 and 1963 were amended in the Mental Health System Act under President Jimmy Carter.

"The Mental Health Systems Act of 1980 (MHSA) was United States legislation signed by President Jimmy Carter, which provided grants to community mental health centers. In 1981, President Ronald Reagan, who had made major efforts during his Governorship to reduce funding and enlistment for California mental institutions, pushed a political effort through the U.S. Congress to repeal most of MHSA. The MHSA was considered landmark legislation in mental health care policy." So, what was included in the original plan by President Carter?

As noted in the official record from the Jimmy Carter Presidential Library:

"The Mental Health System Act placed special emphasis "on the care and treatment of chronic mental illness to ensure that mental health support and aftercare services are available at the community level."[143] It allowed for federal grant money for children, adolescents, and the elderly--all target demographics of the Commission. It strengthened services to the poor in both rural and urban center areas. Additionally, there was authorization in place for grants to nonprofit community mental health centers in order to give appropriate levels of mental health care. Oversight was set in place for persons who had to remain inpatient, with the emphasis that it would be in the "least restrictive settings" possible.[144] When patients were released, they were to be informed of "available community-based facilities and programs" with the caveat that these were to be adequately staffed and funded with programs to provide help and support.[145] It still included the rape prevention and control section added in the House in 1979. A part of particular significance was the Patients' Bill of Rights, Section 501, laying out what a person undergoing treatment could expect of their medical team, why it was appropriate, and what rights they had beyond this, including accessibility, confidentiality, and the right to assert their grievances."[146]

All of this was changed with the election of President Ronald Reagan, who, in 1981, repealed most of the Mental Health Systems Act of 1980.

Election night in 1980 came less than a month after the Mental Health Systems Act was signed into law. By the following summer, it was gone—repealed under the Omnibus Budget Reconciliation Act of 1981, one of President Ronald Reagan's first major legislative moves. The shift wasn't just bureaucratic; it marked a philosophical retreat. Reagan, who as governor of California had already shown a willingness to defund mental health programs—at times with tragic consequences—brought that same mindset to Washington. Mental health care was among the first casualties of his budget cuts.

The new law didn't just undo recent progress; it erased nearly two decades of federal commitment to community-based care, including the Community Mental Health Act of 1963. Only one piece of the 1980 legislation survived, Section 501, the Patients' Bill of Rights, a symbolic gesture of compassion left standing amid the cuts. What had been designed as an integrated system of support was reduced to block grants handed off to states, with funding slashed and accountability scattered. What followed was not just a change in policy but a quiet unraveling of a promise to treat mental health as a shared societal obligation rather than an individual burden.[147]

In addition to the loss of services to help diagnose, facilitate, and resolve Mental Health issues, people suffering from mental health issues also had to deal with the stigma surrounding mental health. Even if the care were available, people would not seek help because of a fear of being labeled. In "The Stigma of Mental Disorder: A millennia-long history of social exclusion and prejudices," Wulf Russler writes, "Research on stigmatization involves a specialized discipline of social science that broadly overlaps with attitude research in social psychology. A scientific concept on the stigma of mental disorders was first developed in the middle of the 20th century, first theoretically and eventually empirically in the 1970s. The book Stigma: Notes on the Management of Spoiled Identity, published in 1963 by the American sociologist Erwin Goffman, laid the foundation for stigma research as a scientific discipline and described how stigmatized persons deal with the challenge.

There is no country, society or culture where people with mental illness have the same societal value as people without a mental illness.

Several years later, an essay by Thomas Scheff triggered much discussion as he controversially described mental disorders as being merely the consequence of a labeling process. Scheff's idea was later modified by Bruce Link, who differentiated the various steps in adopting the role of a mentally ill person. The first step in labeling the mentally ill would include societal standards and norms, and the impact of deviating from these: sufferers increasingly withdraw from social interactions to avoid negative reactions, thereby reducing their participation in society and normal life. This social retreat and isolation diminishes self-esteem and, in turn, increases vulnerability to psycho-social stress. As such, the social networks of the mentally ill are usually very small and restricted." [148]

As kids, we would call a kid that acted out "crazy" or say "loco" while twirling our fingers around our ear. We would joke with each other and say things like "He/She is one fry short of a happy meal", "They're not playing with a full deck", "Their momma must have dropped them on the head as a child" and similar jokes. We would make these jokes as children, not understanding the full psychological weight these jokes may have had on the psyche of the listener. Dr. Farrell writes about how men tease each other as an act of bonding, or in his words, "The exchange of wit-covered put-downs is boys' and men's unconscious way of training each other to handle the criticism it takes to become successful."[149] I have written about the bullying aspect of this previously, and I will speak more about the empathetic side in the upcoming chapters. At this point, I will note that these types of put-downs also lead to negative self-image in boys and men. Multiple studies prove the link between bullying, teasing, eating disorders and psychosomatic problems.

In the metadata study "Bullied Children and Psychosomatic Problems: A Meta-analysis," the authors conclude, "The association between being bullied and psychosomatic problems was confirmed. Given that school bullying is a widespread phenomenon in many countries around the world, the present results indicate that bullying should be considered a significant international public health problem."[150] I believe that there is a line, albeit thin, between bullying and good-natured teasing. Sammy Davis Jr. once said after his time as "Man of the Hour" on the "Dean Martin Celebrity Roast "TV show, "I'm honored to have people I respect make fun of me. It's because the day they stop making fun of you is the day they no longer give a damn about you."[151]

The great Don Rickles,"The Merchant of Venom" or "Mr. Warmth," was known for heckling any and everyone in the crowd. Sinatra, Dean Martin, Sammy, the President, Ali, Chamberlain, Lucille Ball, Ruth

Buzzy, DeNiro, it did not matter who you were, he would heckle you. It was an honor to be heckled by him. He was also known as one of the humblest and more good-natured men in comedy. Mr. Rickles really cared about people and humanity, and his jokes were part of an act. He would end his shows thanking all of the people who helped him get to where he was and talk about his heart and true love for people. In one of his last stage appearances at the Spike TV "One Night Only - An All Star Comedy Tribute to Don Rickles" in May 2014 Mr. Rickles said "What I say to all of you, I picked up a style of working in tough clubs and people making fun and yelling up and so forth and I started to pick on people, always with love. My heart never had a bit of hatred in it, never had a bit of any kind of feeling of anti-, whatever they were, black, green, yellow, I didn't care. I only respected them. And I think the audience knew that."[152] I write this to show that there is a contrast to the art of comedy, which can be good natured, and a way of bridge building, which can be humanitarian, and the depth of despair and trauma that unchecked, biased insults can cause. One can see insults as part of the culture of acceptance, but we must ensure that this is done with permission and understanding, and respect, as Mr. Rickles did.

So where are we now? What is the current condition of men's mental health in America?

Prior to sharing this data, I would like to also point out that with sensitive topics such as mental health, domestic partner violence, verbal abuse, mental health, etc., it is important to acknowledge that many men do not disclose or acknowledge that they may currently suffer from or have been victims of these issues at some point in their lives. These are human issues requiring the same light to be shone on these issues in male circles and communities as they are in female circles and communities. Society must do more to allow men the ability to stand and be counted in the reporting, so that all can get a fuller picture of how men are being affected. All persons that find themselves in situations that they have not consented to, should be believed and given all required support to be made whole.

If you would like to report an instance of intimate partner or domestic violence, please call: ***National Domestic Violence Hotline - 1-800-799-7233***

The Suicide and Crisis Lifeline - also used for mental health emergencies - 988

If you need immediate help, please get in touch with a trusted family member or loved one, and if one is not available, contact 911 and request help for a mental health emergency. Be specific, let the operator know that you want a trained mental health counselor, EMT or Fire Department to assist you, or ask for an alternate number to call for help. The police departments in our nation are trained to protect people and may be overwhelmed if they are focusing on mental health emergencies. It is best for all involved that professionals trained in mental health counseling are the first responders, with law enforcement in place to protect the public and allow the experts to do their jobs. If you have taken any psychoactive substances, please let the responders know what was taken so that they can best help you.

The Statistics

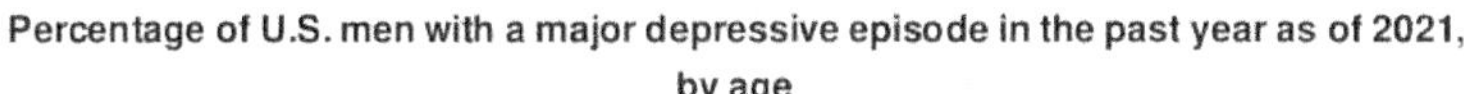

Percentage of U.S. men with a major depressive episode in the past year as of 2021, by age

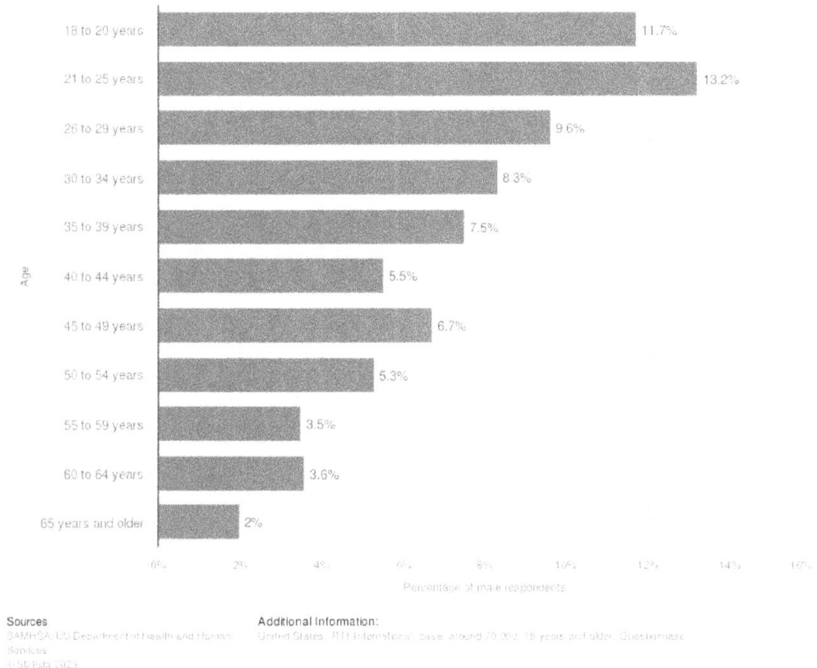

Percentage of U.S. me with a major depressive episode in the past year as of 2021

by age

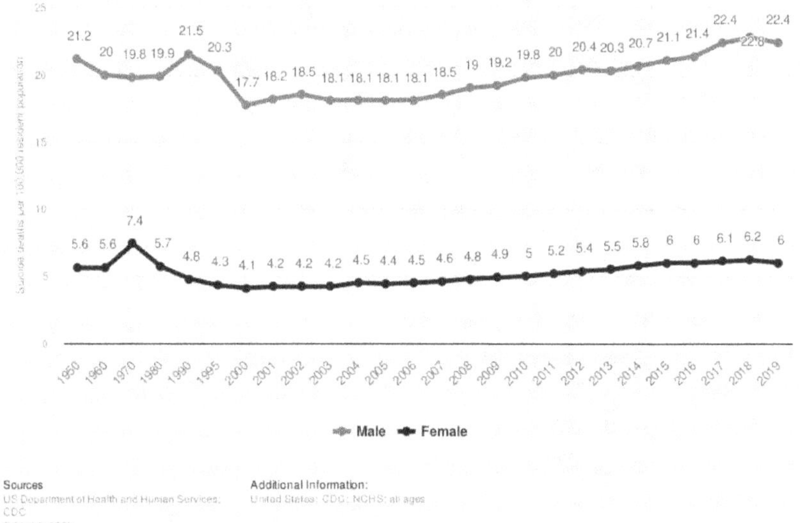

Death by suicide per 100,000 resident population in the US - 1950 to 2019

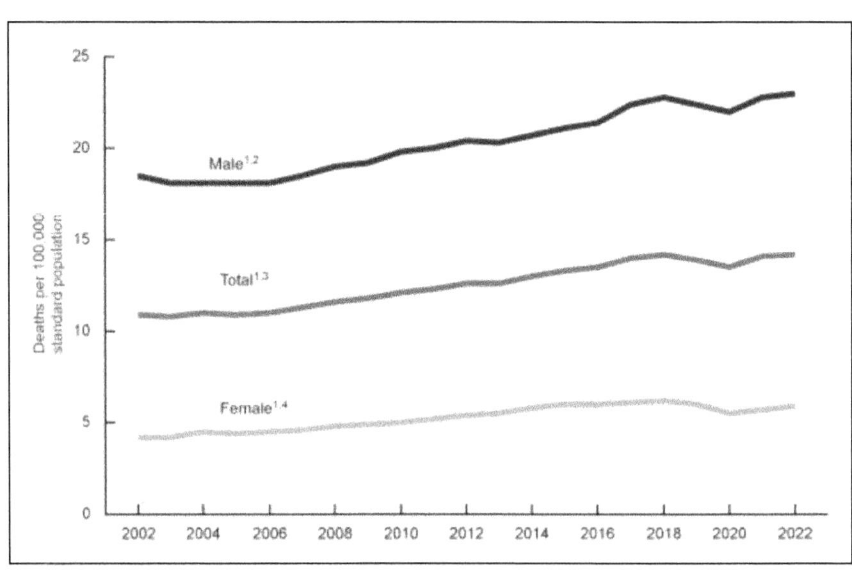

Age adjusted Suicide rates by sex United States

Opioid death rate between men and women in the US

For specific drugs, and after controlling for the sex-specific rate of drug misuse, the researchers found that the overall rates of drug overdose death by sex from 2020-2021 were:

- **Synthetic opioids (e.g., fentanyl):** 29.0 deaths per 100,000 people for men, compared to 11.1 for women

- **Heroin:** 5.5 deaths per 100,000 people for men, compared to 2.0 for women

- **Psychostimulants (e.g., methamphetamine):** 13.0 deaths per 100,000 people for men, compared to 5.6 for women

- **Cocaine:** 10.6 deaths per 100,000 people for men, compared to 4.2 for women[153]

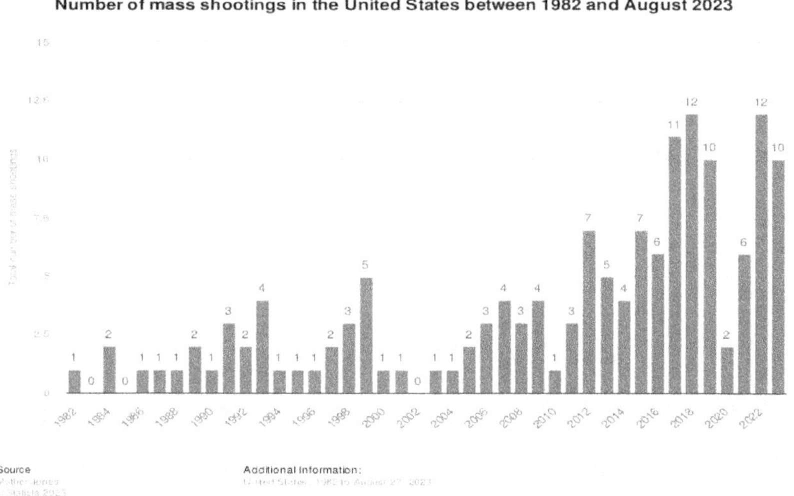

Number of mass shootings in the United States between 1982 and August 2023

Number of mass shootings in the United States between 1982 and August 2023 [154]

Non Suicidal Self-Injury (NSSI)

There have been multiple studies that take on the subject of Non Suicidal Self-Injury. A majority of the studies show that females are greatly affected by NSSI than men. In the study "Characterizing gender differences in non-suicidal self-injury: Evidence from a large clinical sample of adolescents and adults," the authors note the discrepancy in the number of female and male patients entered into the study. The ratio was as follows: "The full sample included 401 males (11.97%) and 2950 females (88.03%). Patients were primarily non-Hispanic white (84.44%), with a mean age of 17.80. Most patients were under the age of 18 at admission (76.24%). There were no significant differences between male and female patients with respect to age (in years and dichotomized into adolescent/adult groups) or ethnicity."[155] The authors of the study also provide a breakdown of the types of self-harm inflicted by the study participants as well as their potential disorders/afflictions. The takeaway from the study is that more research is needed to fully understand how NSSI affects men. One of the major takeaways is how often men would not divulge abuse at the same rate as women would, nor the effects of how NSSI impacts their lives. It is a fascinating study, especially when you view it in the context of volunteerism and how critical open and honest participation is to helping scientists find problems in society and help find solutions.

The information and data provided show that men can and do suffer from mental health challenges, which can be caused by genetics, physical or emotional trauma, and just day-to-day living. The world is a rough place, and it is harder when you see no path forward, nor see a purpose for yourself or that your life matters. The image that men have of masculinity in our society does not make life easy to tap in to your humanity. This idea does not make it easy for men to discuss their feelings, emotions, insecurities, feelings of helplessness or anger without them feeling as though they are less of a man; a lesser value to society. If you are a man with no purpose and all you see in your sphere of influence is the world attacking men, then your choices are to either fight or flight. Hurt People, Hurt People. When people are hurting, they may not have, nor be aware of, the tools available to help them deal with the pain. When I was younger and I struggled with abuse, the church was my solace. Church was a place I could go where I believed that the weight of my worries would go into God's hands. It was the tool that I had available at the time to help me through my trauma. Church can be a tool to help calm one's mind and find a sense of purpose; we also need to pair this with science based counseling and therapy. Counseling and therapy can stand on their own without the Church, and it is important to make that distinction. The goal is to help people find a way to live in the here and now and live their fullest, most satisfying lives.

Why do hurt people hurt people? Dr. Claire Jack, in her article "6 Reasons Some People Hurt the Ones They Love...and what you can do if you're on the receiving end." in Psychology Today writes "Low Empathy.., Self-Dislike.., Low Self Esteem.., They have an Agenda.., They Enjoy Inflicting Pain on Others.., They attracted you because you are Easily Hurt."[156]

As you read each of these lines, take the time to think of someone you hurt for a reason linked to one of these causes. We have all had moments we are not proud of where we hurt people who did not deserve it.

- *Low Empathy* - Empathy is being able to see someone else's point of view and/or "put yourself in someone else's shoes". It is the art of taking a step back and realizing you are not the only person being affected by a situation, and learning how to do and be better for the sake of the relationship.

- *Self-Dislike* - Self-hate or self-loathing, the path to destruction, where you take everyone and everything down with you.

- *Low Self-Esteem* - Devaluing oneself, who they are and the things they do. If you have no value in your own words, then what you say may not matter to you, but it does to those who love and value you.

- *They have an agenda* - When a person puts plans into motion to hurt another for their own pleasure or gain.

- *They enjoy inflicting pain on others* - This is a bit more heavy where, in lieu of having a plan behind their actions, they just do it to do it. The agent of chaos

- **They attracted you because you are Easily Hurt** - Bullying. Bullies seek out the weak to make themselves feel strong. [157]

So, the question becomes, how do we solve these social, emotional, and environmental systems that affect the mental health and lives of men?

Societal

Mental Health Care needs to be included in the discussion to help find solutions to societal issues surrounding guns, the unhoused, the unemployed (or underemployed), the uneducated, low income, opioid addiction, sexual harassment, equity and equality. Many of our societal issues stem from the lack of available Mental Health Care. We are humans, and each and every one of us furthers the future of humanity. In the summer of 2023, I had a conversation with a group of women who were stranded at my Playa parents' RV during the Burning Man "Mudpocalypse" of 2023. We talked about the word "Deserve" and its meaning to humanity. After listening to them speak, I realized that the word deserves should be used in the universal context of what we all deserve as humans. We are humanity, the good, the bad, the ugly. Every day we wake up to contribute to this singular time in human existence. We deserve all that humanity has to offer. As humanity strives to meet its potential, we should strive to kindle a zeal in others to further what humanity can become. After this conversation, I had a synchronistic experience with one of my campmates when I went to tell her about the experience I just had at my parent's RV. Coincidentally, she had written a poem the night of the "Mudpocalypse", prior to our conversation with her about the definition of deserve.

That night she had written:

You Deserve

By Natasha Pritchett[158]

  — Honesty

  — Warmth

— Understanding

— Patience

— Accountability

— Affection

— Humor

— Intelligence

— Play

— Sexuality

— Thoughtfulness

— Openness

These are all of the qualities included in my definition of humanitarian love, articulated more beautifully than I could have written. This was one of the many moments of synchronicity I have experienced in the course of writing this book.

The mental health questions have to be addressed by scientists, social workers, and our elected representatives, which includes a national conversation. The start would be to create laws that go beyond the Mental Health Systems Act of 1980. The mechanism to get to this point requires extensive thought and continual improvement and must be in step with the mental health community's recommendations and results proven treatments. The result should be a system where anyone seeking help can get the help they need without worry of stigma or cost. These are two of the biggest barriers to requesting or seeking help. Stigma about mental health continues to be a hindrance to this day. Society has taken steps to make therapy "hip", but it can still be cost-prohibitive. Many insurances still do not cover mental health care or therapy. Patients should be allowed to foster relationships with their therapists to help them fight through the daily struggles of life. Society needs to change the male perspective of forced self-absorption of feelings, to one that acknowledges the benefits of men being communicative and open. The various media outlets, movies, podcasts, TV, newspapers, etc., can be at the forefront of this movement. Men have to do a better job at listening and encouraging other men to seek counseling when they realize a friend is in need of help. Men should also be willing to join studies that help increase data gathering and funding for studies that will help society make better laws and programs to treat mental health concerns. TV shows like "Shrinking" are helping to introduce men to the concept of beneficial therapy.

Society has to increase the profile and importance of mental health care professionals. Our society will need more health care and social workers to treat the influx of men who are looking for help and treatment. The influx becomes real once the stigma of therapy is released from the vice grip of masculinity. In "The stigma of mental disorders: A millennia-long history of social exclusion and prejudices," Rossler writes, "there are three general approaches that we can use to reduce stigma and discrimination: information/education about mental illness; protest against unfair descriptions of mental illness; and direct contact with the mentally ill. Three "channels" are used to mediate these strategies: mass media, opinion leaders and persons of trust."[159] Mass media, opinion leaders and persons of trust are the vehicles to help minimize and eliminate the stigma behind mental health care. I would add to that the understanding and empathy in understanding that we are all humans, we are the dichotomy of strong and frail; we need to learn how to better deal with our emotions and support the understanding that self-healing, self-care, and forgiveness are how we move forward for ourselves and humanity.

Behavioral

Once a man realizes what he is doing to others, he will either play further into it or stop. There is a weight on the shoulders of men that requires that they be strong and tough and not let the pain influence them. This does not always happen. When men are hurt, we hurt and hurt others. Our pride and personal ego are affected by every "No" we hear. We are taught that we are dominant and need to be as such, in both our emotions and in our lives. This is in contradiction to being human. All humans can be strong when needed, and all humans suffer from pain and hurt. We can also be happy and content with our lives. Those are options that are not always given to us. The "manly" or masculine way of resolution is usually how men are taught to react. As men, we need to both seek out therapy and to also hold each other accountable for our actions and thoughts. We should seek out ways to be better communicators with our partners and our friends. This will allow us to better help those who need help while shielding them from the shame of seeking help. We do better by helping each other. Men should also be willing to seek the help of other men to help a man who is clearly in distress and/or in need of assistance. We cannot continue to live in this fake bubble of not seeing the pain that the other person is in. We need to share with each other and help each other.

Through mentorship, leadership, and understanding we can help each of us become better people, which is a continual process. We deserve to be loved and should love each other, as well as address the humanity of that love, and what we deserve. If I suffer and pain is in my heart, I want my brother to reach out and tell me it will be alright and help me find a positive solution that will reinforce my humanity as well as aid in my well-being. Am I my brother's keeper?! Yes, we all are!!

Technological

As more and more men seek help, more technologies should be adopted to help men build lasting friendships with other men. The stigma of homosexuality and male closeness prevent men from creating long-lasting and loving relationships. When I lived in Japan, I noticed that young boys would hold other boys' hands and sit in each other's laps, and share a closeness that I had not seen in America. I found out later that one of the reasons why this was possible was because of how taboo homosexuality is in Japan. It is similar to what I have seen in Muslim societies. I was recently reading a Reddit page where the question was asked, "Are there Gay bars in the Middle East?" One of the responders wrote, "Women are for childbearing, Men are for fun." I will address the first part of this statement in the next chapter, but I want to emphasize the bonding aspect of this comment. Eliminating the stigma of homosexuality in male culture, especially in America, would allow for more open and honest discussions and friendships with other men. Apps and websites could be created that are dedicated to men finding friendships with other men, or men's groups. Create in men, communities around video games, or other shared technologies, that will encourage met to create tight knit bonding circles; similar to how women are more naturally able to create tight-knit women's circles.

Telehealth has been transformative in giving men and women access to life-saving mental health care. The pandemic has allowed for this form of mental health care to flourish. There are different needs and methods for consideration in creating an overarching technological solution. If you need to speak with a person, there should be an app for that, similar to "Be My Eyes." When Men are in need of help, they can click the app and immediately speak with another man who has been trained to listen and counsel or kick the conversation over to an accredited professional. This is a similar strategy that the Black Rock Ranger Green Dots use then they are helping someone in need of emotional support. Reddit also has a page for men to discuss mental health and how to be a better man. If you feel like you need to just vent and talk about it later, there's an app for that as well. Toastmasters is a program that I have used to help express my ideas and receive feedback in a positive and affirming way. This is a way for men to learn active listening skills, leadership skills, and have a chance at building communal bonds.

As these technologies prove themselves more and more useful, more companies will invest in these forms of treatment. This is why the government must play a role in helping to modulate the prices for these services to make them affordable so that every person has the ability to reach out without fear of crushing debt. We must focus more on the fact that mental challenges are a part of the human experience. These are conditions that many have lived with throughout human history, and it is important to see the resolution as a human right. There is a place for capitalism; however, the greater good of humanity should work alongside it. Every company has the right to make money and pay its employees and shareholders fairly, and just as they move humanity forward, we must always remember that all we create is a reflection of our humanity and human existence.

On a personal note, I want to discuss two other points – physical fitness and acknowledging each other. I can attest to the benefits of exercising and its link to mental health. I have found that when I do not exercise for over a month, I begin to feel the weight of life. Running, cycling and swimming allow me to reflect on things that are on mind and the time I spend exercising is almost like meditating. In the metadata study "Physical Activities and Incident Depression: A Meta-Analysis of Prospective Cohort Studies." The authors find the following: "People who were more physically active were less likely to experience depression than those who were less active. This protective link between physical activity and mental health held true for young people, adults, and older adults alike. The benefits were seen across different parts of the world and were consistent whether depression was measured by screening tools or formal diagnoses. Overall, staying physically active appears to lower the risk of developing depression across ages and regions."[160]

When I was younger I used to hate when other black men would call me brother. At the time I didn't understand the nuance of that word. Over time, after returning from Japan, I learned to embrace my identity as a black man more and started also using the term brother. I understood the bond of shared experience and trauma built into that word. I also noticed that white men were using this term as well. They would use it when speaking to me at times. I thought it odd that they were also calling me brother, yet over time I understood that they also have a shared experience as men in this world. I now use the term in all my interactions with other men. For me it is a way of me acknowledging to them that they are seen.

Chapter Summary

This chapter asks us to take a clear look at how masculinity has been shaped by the world we inherited and how that world has often failed men and boys. From cultural icons to social expectations, we explore how pressure, silence, and emotional suppression have created a real sense of crisis for many modern men. Together we walk through the ways these patterns developed and how they continue to shape the lives of boys who are trying to find their place. The chapter closes by reminding us that redefining masculinity is not a solo act but a shared project. We do this by listening, learning, and working with each other to create a version of masculinity rooted in humanity rather than fear or performance.

Main Points

- Masculinity has been shaped by historical forces, cultural expectations, and outdated ideals that no longer serve modern men or boys.

- Men and boys are experiencing a crisis of identity that comes from emotional suppression, shifting social roles, and the absence of meaningful guidance.

- Redefining masculinity requires honesty, empathy, and collective work so that men can develop healthier identities rooted in humanity rather than performance.

Chapter 6

Redefining Masculinity -

Mature and Immature Masculinity:

How We Save Ourselves

We are finally at the section of this book that has been haunting me for the past 11 years. It is difficult to start this section because I still have misgivings about whether or not I should be writing this book. I spoke with a good friend of mine recently and told her about my misgivings. She is one of the first people I have spoken to about how much this weighs on me and the specific things that weigh on me. She encouraged me to move forward and that I am being too hard on myself. It was another lesson in the myriads of synchronistic moments I continue to have in these last few years.

What is Mature are Immature Masculinity?

Immature Masculinity

Is the trap society has laid out for men, telling them what masculinity is and what is expected of a man, with no care for their humanity. They are intertwined with the concept and notion of the Alpha male. I alone dominate, not we; All is mine, not ours. Immature Masculinity is not self-reflective; it follows the needs of the body, not the soul, and it lashes out and hurts others to feel a sense of empowerment. It sees power as the highest level of masculinity and looks to hold power over others. They lead for themselves and care only for themselves, without any reflective thought for others. Toxic masculinity is a hallmark trait of Immature Masculinity. Blamelessness and rejection of ownership for one's influence and actions.

Mature Masculinity

Mature Masculinity is when a man sees themselves as the individual, as well as being a greater part of humanity. A mature man is self-reflective and self-aware. The first question is not only how it benefits me, but also how it benefits others; it is the right thing to do? Mature Masculinity involves asking the best out of yourself and others, while understanding how to help people be the better versions of themselves. As a protector, you protect the right to a thought or idea, you protect the right to exist, basic human rights are under your protective care - life, liberty, and the pursuit of happiness. Mature Masculinity is rooted in the base nature of humanity, empathy for others and a desire for life. We work for each other and the group. Our base needs are those which ensure the survival of humanity. We do this through inner reflection, understanding of our place in the world, how we affect others through our presence and how we can continue to foster the forward advancement of humanity.

Toxic Masculinity

In a New York Times opinion piece, Maya Salam writes, "What does 'toxic masculinity,' or 'traditional masculinity ideology,' mean? Researchers have defined it, in part, as a set of behaviors and beliefs that include the following:

- Suppressing emotions or masking distress

- Maintaining an appearance of hardness

- Violence as an indicator of power (think: "tough-guy" behavior)

In other words, Toxic masculinity is the end result of teaching boys that they can't express emotion openly; that they have to be "tough all the time"; that anything other than that makes them "feminine" or weak. It does not mean that men are inherently toxic."[161]

During the course of this book, we discussed the history of masculinity, the standard definition of masculinity, how men have been affected by masculinity, as well as how to reviewing some potential solutions of the basic societal problems men are challenged with in society.

I have spent the last 20 years of my life working in the construction industry. I have worked with some of the hardest, roughest, toughest types of men to walk this plane of existence. I learned more about masculinity from them than I had in the 25 years. I also learned about the mask that they use to shield their true emotions. I became close to many of the men I worked with. From project managers to superintendents, engineers and architects, owners, developers; from workers to foremen, I became friends and engaged with them all. I had seen examples of both Mature Masculinity and Immature Masculinity, and these examples helped me question the true definition of masculinity and the definition that society burdens men with. The pressure, the pain, the need to show resilience under pressure, the fear, the heroism, the camaraderie, the love, the hate, the smallest of people and the greatest of people, and how we built monuments to the sky, which act as testaments to the will of humanity.

It is not my place to judge others. As humans, we all experience pain and trauma, which affects the way we interact with people and how we live our lives. Toxic Masculinity is the result of society's blueprint of masculinity. Holding back emotions and feelings is what is seen as being masculine. A leader who shares their feelings and talks about the hardships and pains they go through on a daily basis isn't what our society wants to see from a leader. They want clear, efficient, effective leadership. They don't want to know about his troubles; they want to know that you are fixing their problems. There is no concern for humanity in their expectations, and there is no concern for humanity in the response. Is it fair to define something as toxic when societal pressures force men to live within these restraints on their humanity? There is a difference between self-inflicted hurt and hurting others. Many of the examples of Toxic Masculinity are described in how others were affected by it. This is where the description of Immature Masculinity can be used instead.

A man who lashes out in anger to hurt another person is showing Immature Masculinity. Mature Masculinity is taking the time to understand the situation, the people in the situation, their own power dynamic and asking how best to resolve a concern effectively, using empathy and active listening. The fact that society has these norms and pressures exerted on men is also Toxic, Social Toxicity. This should also be part of the conversation when discussing Toxic Masculinity. There is no effect without a cause. The beauty about humans is that we can change and become better. It is important to see the dichotomy in Toxic Masculinity as well as the human element in the victim and the perpetrator. This is the only way to heal and move forward.

Chapter 7

The New Definition - Humanity and the battle for hearts and minds

I have immature masculine tendencies. I continue to work on them and try to do better. Mature Masculinity is not a final destination; it is a metric and standard that men should look to hold themselves and other men accountable to. We cannot depend on society to look out for our best interests. We have families and people who count on us to be our best selves. We owe it to ourselves to be the best person, with the understanding that we are human and fallible; we can be forgiving and can forgive. We are treated the way we allow the world to treat us, we should expect better for ourselves and of society. We start this journey with us.

Mature Masculinity - Respect

If a group of men are hanging out and a woman walks by, someone may catcall her. This action creates a response paradigm where she can either ignore or respond to the cat call. In most instances, a woman would walk away and pay no mind, but that humiliation is still there (in NYC, you will be told things about your momma that you didn't know and you might get knocked out... Love my city). Some men believe she "likes it" or "wants it"; they believe it makes her feel wanted. That would be a great analysis if we had mind-reading devices hooked up to every woman who walks by. What may seem like an innocent encounter has repercussions on the victim's psyche. There is no self-reflection by the perpetrator. That is Immature Masculinity. Mature Masculinity would require a higher moral ground.

Mature Masculinity is in quickly stamping down the cat call and telling them to "STOP" while creating a teaching moment. "This is not who we are. We are and can be better than this." Some might say, "That's a contradiction, you say we should express ourselves and they condemn us for doing so." You have to ask yourself, "What is my intention? Why am I doing this?" If you really want her to know that you think she is beautiful, then why not just let her know? There is no shame in being vulnerable enough to let her know in a way that isn't performative. Is her attention the end goal? Are you moving with purpose, or are you doing it because it's what you believe is expected of you, a show of your manhood? The mature or humanistic goal is to make efforts to build connections with people and build each other up. This should be done with no regard to how the results benefit you. Selflessness and self-expression are acts of Mature Masculinity. Moving with purpose and respect, are acts of Mature Masculinity.

One trait that I have always appreciated among the men and women I have worked with, is the ability to respect each other regardless of the difficulties we have faced. We may not always see eye to eye, but there is a shared comfort in knowing that we are both building something and are in the concrete together. I once had a shouting match with a co-worker at a construction site. We were yelling and shouting at each other; it was brutal. I was junior to him, an Assistant Project Manager. He was a more senior superintendent. We shouted and yelled at each other because we were both stressed from the job, and I didn't think he was taking the job as seriously as I was. From his vantage point, he thought I was being too aggressive on the job when there were a lot of parts at play that I didn't fully understand at the time. I have had a few similar instances earlier in my career; my style and stance changed with experience and maturity. I did not know how to handle the situation at the time, and we went at each other.

I realize now that, outside of the stress and need to get the job done, I shouted at him because I felt I could do so. I may or may not have been in the right, but what I displayed was Immature Masculinity. I was able to amend our relationship and continue moving forward, and he is a great guy whose career I have been following ever since. When faced with a similar situation with another superintendent, I didn't feel I could use the same tactic for fear of losing my job. I realized that I had to kick it up to my boss. I may not have been able to change the person's behavior; however, it did not mean that I was not capable of doing my job. I had to learn to separate what I can do and how I can affect a situation and maximize those efforts. When you are young, being taken seriously can be a very sensitive subject; It was for me. I had to let the project executive do his job and understand that I cannot control everything. I cannot force people to care as much as I did. What I failed to understand at the time is how respect, leadership, and accountability work together to build success. Mature Masculinity is in allowing others to take on their share of the burden, as well as being able to take a step back and figure out the best solution.

When I became a direct manager for the first time, I read a lot of management books that focused on responsibility, accountability, empathy and motivation. "How to Win Friends and Influence People," by Dale Carnegie, is a book that has changed my life and my relationships. "How to

Win Friends and Influence People" as well as "Ultimate Ownership: How Seals Train and Win" by Jacko Winock, are books that I would include in the Mature Masculinity starter pack. Both books discuss how to relate with people and groups; understanding your goals and objectives and how to get there; understanding who you are, what power you have available to get to your goal and how to help and encourage people along the way to achieving success. These books also discuss when/if failure occurs, how to take responsibility, and become better. Reading books reminds me of the side-scrolling video games I grew up playing, like "River City Ransom," where you would go into a store and read a book and gain a new ability or increased power.

Life experience can be gained through the experience of others. When you are in a teachable moment, it is important to take the time to be present in that moment, take time to think of the best path forward and how it can make you better. This is how we show respect to ourselves and others. It is ok to get angry or upset, it's a natural human response. Maturity is recognizing these feelings and taking the time to let your thoughts, not feelings, dictate how you respond. We should strive to be cool like Fonzie. We all get triggered. Sometimes, we have to take a step back and allow the situation to wash over us to help find the best path forward. A book that tackles these modes of thinking is "Thinking Fast and Slow" by Daniel Kahneman. This book gives us detailed insight into our immediate *(system 1)* and long term *(system 2)* processing. When you know more about the 'why', you can do more to change your behavior. "Knowing is half the battle."

I have worked with many hard edged and stubborn people. These are people who believe that there is nothing you can tell them that they haven't already learned. True intelligence is knowing what you know and also understanding what you do not know. Each opportunity to learn from others makes you a better person. There is a saying we use often in construction, "You learn something new every day". Many of us love working in construction because of the breadth of knowledge and understanding gained and required to work in this field. The diverseness of people and backgrounds, our closeness to the edge of technology and human advancement, and the shared feeling when a building tops out (completion of roof slab) or project completion, are aspects of construction that create a shared sense of accomplishment. How does one show respect and give respect to people who are unwilling to be team players? I like to call it the Asshole Paradox.

When dealing with someone of this nature, you have the options of either reacting to them, reacting with them, or staying silent. Reacting to them requires deft and skill that can blur and cross the lines of mature and Immature Masculinity. If your goal is to protect others from potential harm caused by the antagonist, then you are naturally aligned with Mature Masculinity. If the goal is to bring about humiliation, then that is Immature Masculinity. A protective reaction requires self-reflection, thoughtfulness and understanding. A chessboard needs the pieces laid out before any game can begin. In chess, once your opponent makes their first move, you can then decide on the response and the type of game you want to play. Then, as each piece moves towards the center, strategies can be developed to gain advantages to achieve one's goal. If we do not begin this path with mindfulness, thoughtfulness, self-reflection and from a place of respect, we ourselves are at risk of being the Asshole, hence the paradox. One additional tool I had picked up while training to be a Black Rock Ranger is the technique of matching someone's intensity while speaking with them. When you decide to confront the situation, you can begin the conversation by matching their intensity. Mirroring their actions lets them see how they are acting and they may sober up to their own behavior. Please note that this works more when you have an established relationship and there is a dynamic where the person will understand that you are coming from a place of love, caring and understanding. A relationship has to be established for this to work, and that comes with mutual respect, understanding and a willingness to work on the relationship, productively.

Once you feel the time is right, start the conversation their behavior and be factual. Be empathetic if they open up about the root causes of their behavior. If you begin with humanity, you never have to enter into the paradox. Be open and human with them. If they are unwilling to be open or be part of the solution, then set the terms and boundaries and stand by them. If you need help or feel that the process may cause physical harm to your person, then have the conversation in public and with people you trust. Always lead and end in respect and be mindful of the power dynamic; respected peers, those with close relationships, or mentor/mentee power dynamics can have these kinds of conversations without great concern. If it is a workplace conversation, HR should be informed of the conversation to get their thoughts on how the dynamic should be handled. This protects the company and the workers.

When met with the options of reacting to the antagonist, reacting with the antagonist, or staying silent; it is important to understand the following about each course of action: the first interaction is to protect and defend; the second is to work with the person to find a solution to the problem; the third is to do nothing which is far worse and has unintended consequences. Working with them is the best of the three solutions, in my opinion, because it requires that you invest time and be part of the solution. This will develop a greater level of respect between the two parties as well as the outside observer. The conversation starts from the same place of mindfulness, self-reflection, thoughtfulness and respect and uses inclusive and constructive word, like "Us" or "We." We have to be vulnerable for them to be vulnerable with you. Together, you can find a solution and work it out. This strengthens and builds bridges for future conversations and reliance on each other.

The last reaction of saying nothing is to allow the silence of the room to be filled with their voice and echo back their behavior to them. This also allows you time to think about the situation further and try to understand what the trigger was and how to potentially defuse it, if it can be. This solution works best when the power dynamic is from low to high and is followed up with actions that creates collaborative working solution. The resolution will most always require a follow-up with a person who is of the same power dynamic as the antagonist. It is important to keep the peace in these situations. You may have to sit and take in their anger. Do not let their words affect and change who you are. When the conversation is over, be sure to write down both your feelings and the words used so that you can have this available when you present this situation for resolution with a third party. If you immediately respond to them, you put yourself at risk. You want to add arrows to your quiver before going into battle. Immature Masculinity does not respect the person they are speaking to. You are not on their level or and they may not see the humanity in you. Respect requires humanizing someone, seeing them as part of the greater family of humanity. This is why the third party that can help resolve this conflict has to be someone that is respected by both with a similar power dynamic.

Respect is hard to give when bias plays a part in defining others. When we meet people, our brains automatically make assumptions, biased calculations and inferences on who they are before we even speak to them. This is called unconscious bias. Unconscious bias is an evolutionary trait humans evolved to help them quickly determine good from bad. As humans, we have the gift and ability to reprogram our thinking. Psychologically and physically (see the previous chapter on critical thinking). We break the cycle of the Asshole paradox by seeing and respecting the human first and taking the steps to understand them and their viewpoint. They may still be Assholes, but you took the time to show them respect and treat them as humans and try to bring them into the fold of humanity. You can only change yourself and try to influence others through your actions. That is Mature Masculinity.

A Word about Consent

Enthusiastic Consent is a concept that I was introduced to in 2017 when I went on my virgin (solo) trip to Burning Man. The original concept was just consent, which was to ask for a person's permission to engage with them physically. Later it became "enthusiastic consent," to further push the vocalization of consent along with the body language. As a sexual assault survivor, I understand how important it is to maintain ownership of one's body. As a Rotarian (Member of a Rotary Club), while interacting with infringed upon and disenfranchised communities, I came into contact with the concept of consent more and more. After Burning Man, as I started dating again, I would begin to apply the concept of consent during my dates. Some women were familiar with the concept, others were not. In a majority of the situations, if I would ask for consent to hold her hand, give a hug or a kiss, I would be thanked for asking their consent. I was thanked, regardless of their eventual response. I also experienced some negative responses to my request for consent. I once had a woman ask 'what was wrong with me?', she had never had a guy ask for consent, it left me "effeminate" in her eyes. The "effeminate male" link to consent has been the majority of my negative experiences. Consent can be difficult to navigate at times, especially after a relationship has been established. Men should always ask for a person's consent prior to any physical interaction or even an interaction that may be seen in a negative light without context. Consent is also required for the taking and use of someone's image. There is an interesting conversation about how this extends into the public domain and permissions for public photography, which I will not discuss here. It is important to understand the rules and policies of taking public photos and being mindful one's consent when they are the subject of your photo.

Consent is tied to another person's agency. If you are unsure of how to approach someone, ask. The default should be to ask for consent and as time wears on the other party can give their permission to make the request for consent non-obligatory (and even then, when new situations appear, it doesn't hurt to check). Immature Masculinity does not ask for or wait for consent. Immature Masculinity assumes it has the right to the body of another person, more so if they feel they are "owed". The word "STOP" regardless of the tone or vocal variation, said one time, means just that. STOP!!!!! Do not pass go, do not proceed, all tickets are null and void beyond this point. Someone once told me that when a man upsets or rejects a woman's advances, his only worry is that her feelings will get hurt; but when a woman upsets or rejects a man's advances, she is scared that he will kill her. This is not a hyperbolic statement. Time and time again women are reminded of the physical difference between men and women and how this combined with rage, or entitlement, can cause their deaths. Mature Masculinity asks us to take the other into consideration - their needs, their wants, their welfare. Through the act of consent, we learn boundaries and create a protective space for the relationship we are trying to foster. Mature Masculinity also requires that men acknowledge their own ability to give and require consent, as well as their ability to say "STOP". Too many men believe that they are emasculated if they speak out against unwanted advances or touching. Men under report assault and harassment because of societal stigmas, jeering and disapproving eyes of other men. There have been many times where I would hear of a report about a boy being molested by their female teacher, or another female authority figure, and comments from other men would range from "wishing their teachers did that to them" to "how lucky he is." How many young boys are sexually abused by female and male adults and goes underreported or unreported? There was an article in the Daily Beast titled "ISIS Women Accused of Turning Boys as Young as 13 Into a Human Stud Farm" where boys described the following "We are being forced to have sex with the ISIS women, to impregnate them.' Ahmet, 13, and Hamid, 14, told a guard at Camp al Hol in northeast Syria,"[162] In Japan 478 victims of Johnny Kitagawa, a famous Japanese music producer, came forward with allegations of sexual abuse at the hands of Kitagawa and associates.[163] These were young men and boys who were molded and modeled into the next pop stars in Japan and the world.

In the article "The Understudied Female Sexual Predator" by Conor Friedrdorf, he references the peer reviewed paper, "Sexual Victimization Perpetrated by Women: Federal Data Reveal Surprising Prevalence" Co-authored with Andrew Flores and Ilan Meyers, it appears in "Aggression and Violent Behavior" The author's write "But among men reporting other forms of sexual victimization, 68.6% reported female perpetrators,"[164] the paper reports, while among men reporting being made to penetrate, "the form of nonconsensual sex that men are much more likely to experience in their lifetime….79.2% of victimized men reported female perpetrators."[165] I use these examples to point out the need for boys and men to come forward when they are victims of rape, sexual assault, domestic violence and/or intimate partner violence. The more these traumatic experiences are reported, the more society will work to help curb this epidemic for all victims. If you are a survivor of sexual or domestic/intimate partner violence or assault, there are a multitude of programs that will help you find legal and punitive justice. There are programs that will also help you regain the confidence or sense of self lost from these encounters.

Mature Masculinity will not allow another generation of boys and men feel shameful in reporting abuse. This shadow of secrecy among men who have been victims of such abuse has to come to light. Therapy and counseling should be easily accessible to all victims of these types of crimes. In Kendrick Llamar's song "Mother|Sober" he speaks about the subject of molestation and the trauma it causes, even if allegations are unfounded, they can still scar. He also speaks about how these traumas can cause hyper sexualization. He is an advocate for therapy, Mr. Llamar has been instrumental in helping destigmatize therapy.

Perpetrators should also be brought to justice through the process of restorative justice. Many of these people are victims themselves. Hurt people, Hurt people. By advocating for consent, you are giving someone the opportunity to make a decision, giving them the agency to decide how they want to move forward in their lives. This is a human right. In asking consent you recognize the humanity in the other and they acknowledge yours. The answer may not be what you want to hear yet it builds a level of respect on a human level. During the course of asking for consent, the requestor should also be mindful of the power dynamic at play, and make sure all parties feel safe to give an unsolicited, uncompromised response. See Appendix A for a list of services that can help you and someone you love in need of therapy, If you want to report a domestic violence or intimate partner violence please call your local authorities by dialing 911 for immediate help. If you are looking for the strength to protect yourself and other please call

National Domestic Violence Hotline: **1-800-799-SAFE (7233)** or text **START** to **88788**

The Nation Domestic Violence Hotline supports men and women who are survivors of Domestic Violence and Intimate Partner Violence.

Dating

Dating can be a chasm when trying to understand how Mature and Immature Masculinity approach the subject. There is an inherent power imbalance in dating. Both men and women, at some point, hold the reins of power - historically and in relationships. Men have held the reins longer societally and some men continue to hold false expectations of where they are in the pecking order of dating. There are some men that believe that their power and influence is to be rewarded with the best things in life. Sex and women should be part of the prize for male dominance. As women have come into their own, the need for a protector and provider is choice. Today men also have the choice to take on the traditional domestic role at home. As women break glass ceilings and become CEOs and business owners, they are right to want and expect the same access to power that men have had for centuries. We now find ourselves in the era of a shifting power dynamic between men and women in business and in dating.

The societal standard for dating is that the man pays for the first date. Chivalry is a form of peacocking, or performative dance, that men perform to show interest in a woman, to protect a woman's innocence and virtue. This is still performed today and is expected in the dating scene. Mature Masculinity involves recognizing, first, whether you are in an emotional, psychological, and financial position to date. Many of us believe that we are ready to go out and date and may not realize we are not ready. There are many books written on dating and I would invite the reader to do their own research on the topic. Find books that use scientific or evidence based data to support their ideas and writings. During my dating escapades, used information on Love Languages, the NY Times articles on questions that lead to love, and have reviewed books and shows that focus on effective communication. These are the best areas to start on one's dating journey, to understand the types of personalities and beliefs you will encounter. Also ask questions to people who are in healthy relationships, inside and out. It is important to understand what you want to achieve when dating. It is important to be intentional. Mature Masculinity is intentional. If you are only looking for sex or a fling, then you are not ready to date. Many of us do not have great examples of what a good relationship looks like, therefore it is important to speak with others about where you are on your journey and where you want to be.

You are ready to date when you:

1. Know what you, as an individual, need to feel loved and cared for;
2. Know how to express your feelings and can hold civil and open discussion with your partner. This means being vulnerable;
3. Can give your partner what they need to feel loved and cared for. Allow them to be vulnerable;
4. Can listen to them express their feelings and hold civil and open discussions with your partner. A deep level of respect is required to begin a journey with your potential partner.
5. Have a mature understanding of how the physical aspects of a relationship can create a tighter bond, but can also requires dedication by both to the relationship. This includes being open to what they need and them being open to what you need to feel cared for during the physical sides of a relationship.

Not every person is the right one for you. Dating requires understanding who you are and what you want in a partner, as well as understanding what you are willing to live with. People evolve and grow. It is important to find a person that understands that path and can grow with you. Sometimes people grow apart, and that is ok. Sometimes it's the journey that takes us to where we are supposed to be and makes us the person we need to be in that moment.

Not everyone believes in chivalry. I once dated someone that required that I walk on the street side of sidewalk when walking in the street. My experience as a construction manager has taught me that it's more dangerous to walk on the building side than the streetside. Horse drawn carriages aren't running rampant in the streets splashing mud everywhere. As much as I objected to it, internally, I still did it. It was an easy and simple request that I was comfortable obliging. If I had a strong opinion about it I should first reflect internally and understand why I have such a strong opinion. Was there a deeper reason for it? Was it based in ignorance or just me being stubborn? If I did have a strong bias for it then I would need to discuss my feelings with my partner and if they felt they needed this and could not compromise (or a deal breaker) then we should amicably part ways. When you stay in a situation where you feel forced, this can breed contempt and resentment. This is a form of Immature Masculinity. Every day will not be sunshine and rainbows, there will be arguments and hurt feelings. It's the honest discussions during and after that matter. The respect that you show each other during these difficult times are what matters. Some things can be said and can never be unsaid. When dating it is important to understand how your potential partner deals with conflict and if they are able to be self-reflective and self-corrective. Can you and your partner come to a compromise to continue building and strengthening the relationship? Those are questions that Mature Masculinity will ask.

Pimp Johnny Dollar once said "Love the one that loves you." What does that mean? Too many times men find themselves either trying to get into or stay in a relationship with someone that doesn't care for them. This reminds me of the scene in "A Beautiful Mind." There is a bar scene where John Nash realizes that if all of the men went after the most beautiful woman, only one would be successful, if they all went after the other women at the bar, they may all be successful and not have to worry about the most beautiful woman at the bar. The heart wants what the heart wants, I understand this all too well. I spent a good 4 years of my life living that nightmare. I realize now that I put my self-value in others. I burdened them by my want of a relationship, just to help make me feel worthwhile when I already was. I say this with the gift of hindsight. I realize that in those times I was in a place I did not see worth in myself. This is why fellowship with other men and therapy are important tools to self-help and healing. We are all worthy of love, we evolved as social creatures to be part of the cycle of love that is one of the core strengths of humanity. Every time we date, we need to date with intention. Our partner should be the person we can be our most vulnerable selves with. There should be no fear of pain or retribution. We should be each other's peace. Even when we are hurt or moved from that peace, we should also know that we have friends, family, fellowship, and therapy to help us find our way back from the brink. You are not alone.

My last thought on dating is to talk about objectification. Men are not money bags to be used to buy whatever a person wants or needs. Men are not inconveniences that are tolerated for what they can give or buy. Men are not children to cajole, manipulate, or be emasculated for one's enjoyment. Men have feelings, responsibilities, needs, wants, desires, and dreams. Men can be affectionate and need affection. Man can be loved and show love. Men feel pain and desire; lust and rage; hate and despair. Men understand depression and can feel desperation; men can be heroic and feel heroism. Men are not one size fits all, men are sensitive, caring protectors who also deserve to be protected. Men can do all things in the strength of their character and lose it all in the depths of their sorrow. Men are humans and are part of humanity. Now go back to the beginning of this paragraph and replace men with another gender. We are all the same, and this barely touches the magnanimity that is humanity. We need to remember the trees for the forest. It is easy to chop down a forest when you see only the greatness of its expanse and not the individual trees. Each relationship we build is with an individual not a group. Mature Masculinity cherishes the individual, it evaluates and interacts on that basis. Immature Masculinity sees the group and condemns all actions of the singular as that of the group. The whole is the singular in Immature Masculinity; the single is not the whole in Mature Masculinity. Mature Masculinity expects to be seen by others as an individual and discerns the group and the other. In Immature Masculinity their leaders teach them to be prideful and boastful in their immaturity, so that they can take and seize what they perceive they want. The male ego is oppressed by these others. Their thoughts tell them that "they are not us and will never understand our feelings and so we devoid ourselves of feelings and take as we need."

The disciples of Immature Masculinity may even read these words and not recognize themselves. The earth revolves around the sun and sunrise comes once a day, and one may never know if they have their backs always to the sun. The shadows and strings of light that play on the earth are child's play to the glory and majesty that is the sun. It nourishes and leads us to the wonders of the Universe. Humanity is our goal and purpose. It is our Sun. Those who see the group miss out on the humanity of the individual, and we will never understand the individual without understanding Humanity. The ego is in us but does not define us, our humanity, and the will to love and be loved. To remove Immature Masculinity you must push forward on the quests that only Mature Masculinity can offer - Finding yourself; learning self-reflection and using that to change for the better; learning how to love and be loved; remembering, learning and acknowledging that the individual is not the group; giving respect and requiring respect; being open to redefining your values and role in society. All lead to life, all lead to the path of Mature Masculinity.

Sex

In Mature Masculinity, the path towards a sexual relationship begins with the asking of consent. Consent has to be given enthusiastically and by a person of legal age and mental capacity. Mature Masculinity also requires that men understand how important they are in the reproduction process. Your genetic material, when its use is not protected, can affect your future in many ways that you may not think of in those few moments of bliss. Be mindful of who you give your body to. Your body is a temple and your genetic material should ideally be shared with someone that you believe would make a great parent or partner in parenting. Immaturity does not account for how and where you share your genetic material. Immature Masculinity does not care about protection. It is only the pleasure Immature Masculinity seeks and lives for. There is nothing wrong with the pleasure side of sex. It is a wonderful human experience. It is evolution at its finest. Every part of our being is primed for sexual reproduction and the siring of offspring. You can choose to have sex with multiple partners, but ask yourself what is the point? Be honest with yourself as to why you want to. For some of us it's to just feel a connection to someone, something that is brief and intimate. For some it may be the only time they feel any real power or submission in their lives. These are all valuable human feelings and practices when performed with consent and in a mature capacity.

I am not here to Yuck your Yum, I am here to ask you to evaluate your yum. There is a purpose in everything we do, as well as a consequence. Before we decide on how we expend ourselves, we should understand why we want to, and if possible, can we add further value and fulfillment in doing so. If you reflect and find that you like doing it for the sensation and the pleasure of it, then go ahead my friend. Possibly look into other ways that do not involve human interaction if the desire is really based on just the physical need for pleasure. You can also find others that share similar thoughts towards sex but be sure to approach them from a mature viewpoint – they are a part of humanity and have needs, wants, wishes and desires – care should be given and taken. If you need that personal connection, then there is more reflection needed as to the why. This 'why' should be discussed and reflected upon within fellowship with other men, in counseling or in therapy. A person with the ability to become pregnant can decide if they want to proceed with or terminate their pregnancy. No other person can make that decision, except in rare cases. With the ability to become pregnant also comes the right to pursue legal action for custodial and monetary assistance for the child. In Mature Masculinity there lies a deep respect for fatherhood, and an understanding of the path required to raise a mature and well-adjusted participant in humanity. Some people may never be ready to be parents, and some are. Some become ready when the reality of pregnancy sets in, some run from the responsibility. The choice of who we parent with is the only choice we truly have before the child is created.

Once the child is born, raising the child is not an option, it is a responsibility. Either you take care of that responsibility, or the legal system will ensure that you do. If we date with purpose and find a partner that can be our peace, then the path of fatherhood will be a tremendous joy, even if the relationship ultimately runs its course. Immaturity looks out only for its own needs and does not consider the current or future needs of the parents or child. Immaturity only sees the momentary release and not the 5AM feedings, doctor's appointments, sleep training, falls, broken arms, first heartbreak, first, second and third attempts at a driver's license, first dance, graduation, the pain of their first death, the joy of their first child, the need to drop off their children to grandma and grandpa's house before self-implosion, the last words and last breath at the end of a life lived. There is power in the moment, it is your power to give away. It is a seed that plants the future and burrows the path forward for future trees. If you are unsure of the moment or the person you are with, or just want to have fun, use protection. Always carry a condom with you and change it out every 1 to two months or get a new set if you plan to have sex that day. Only use condoms with spermicide. Get tested every three months for all sexually transmitted disease and be supportive of fellow men as they navigate their sex lives. Before any sexual encounter ask yourself "Is an 18 second decision, for 18 minutes of bliss, worth 18 years of lost choices?" *The law of 18.*

I want to leave with this last word and weigh in on the conversation about sex drives. Men have high sex drives. Procreation is part of our evolution, as a species, and with that came sexual behavioral characteristics. Our virility is not a question; it is like the sun rising. A metadata study titled "Sex drive: Theoretical conceptualization and meta-analytic review of gender differences" of over 600,000 participants "The meta-analysis revealed a stronger sex drive in men compared to women, with a medium-to-large effect size, $g = 0.69$, 95% CI [0.58, 0.81]. Men more often think and fantasize about sex, more often experience sexual affect like desire, and more often engage in masturbation than women"[166] It should be noted that even with this study some will argue that there is no common agreement on how to measure sex drive, however the authors used the best information and evidence based criteria for their study.

The use of sex drive is one of the greatest marketing devices that use our evolutionary biases to make money. For men and women these biases are taken advantage of everyday. Mature Masculinity pushes forward the concept that men are humans and are included in the discussion of humanity, we are not just walking penises. Yes, we have high sex drives, however we are more than that. Men need to take back the power from those that exploit us and we should expect more from them. We should expect more from ourselves and expect more from society. Our bodies are not fodder to build bridges to riches and fame. Society needs to have frank and open conversations about sex work. Sex work is not limited to men seeking women, but to all people looking for connection, warmth, and sometimes sex. We deny our evolutions by not talking about sex. Are we truly allowing all people the ability to live out and seek the promise of life, liberty, and happiness.

Before entering this conversation, it is necessary to acknowledge the long history of harm tied to sex work and the ways that harm continues to fall disproportionately on women. Across the world, women are taken, sold, deceived, or forced into lives they never chose. Passports are seized, choices disappear, and entire futures are shaped by fear. This is a global crisis that demands sustained moral, legal, and societal attention.

Human trafficking is a system of coercion and exploitation that affects an estimated 27 million people worldwide. While men and boys are also targeted, women and girls make up the majority of those trafficked for both labor and commercial sex. The consequences are severe. Survivors often lose basic rights, family stability, and, in many cases, their childhoods. Many experience long-term psychological harm, including anxiety, depression, post-traumatic stress disorder, and substance use disorders, alongside high rates of physical and sexual violence. Research consistently shows that women trafficked for sexual exploitation experience profound isolation, heightened fear, and extensive trauma. Some studies identify symptoms consistent with traumatic bonding to abusers, underscoring how trafficking exploits vulnerability and strips individuals of autonomy. These realities make trafficking a central issue in any serious discussion of gender, power, and societal responsibility.

In the paper "The Relationship of Trauma to Mental Disorders Among Trafficked and Sexually Exploited Girls and Women," researchers found that injuries and sexual violence during trafficking were associated with higher levels of PTSD, depression, and anxiety. Longer periods spent in trafficking correlated with increased depression and anxiety, while more time elapsed since leaving trafficking was associated with reductions in depression and anxiety—but not PTSD. These findings highlight the enduring nature of trauma and the deep psychological toll of sexual exploitation.

Understanding this dark reality is essential if we are to have an informed and honest conversation about voluntary sex work. Sex trafficking is not voluntary sex work. Any form of sex work that is not under the explicit, ongoing control of the individual involved is forced sex work. Conflating coercion with consent erases the experiences of victims and undermines meaningful solutions.

Every person deserves the right to decide what happens to their own body and how they choose to live their life. Society has a responsibility to create conditions in which safety is possible, opportunity exists, and dignity is foundational rather than conditional. In many places, women have never been given the space—or the power—to imagine autonomy, let alone practice it. Some were never taught that agency was available to them. Others were never allowed to believe it.

Mature Masculinity recognizes this human truth. It acknowledges the weight of history and the ways power has shaped who is permitted to choose and who is forced merely to survive. It works toward a world in which all people can claim agency and build lives that reflect their own values, hopes, and freedoms. At its core is the belief that life, liberty, and the pursuit of happiness should not be abstract ideals but lived realities. Humanity, at its best, allows people to choose their path and decide how they wish to participate in society. People paint because they love painting; they may also sell their work because there is a market for talent. If a person's genuine passion is sexual expression and they freely choose to earn a living through it, there should be no inherent shame in that choice.

That said, no person or entity should be permitted to profit directly from the exploitation of someone who has chosen sex work. Sexual freedom must be accompanied by strong protections against abuse—for both performers and patrons. Sex workers should be protected under the law, able to work in the safest conditions possible, free from social stigma, discrimination, or fear of persecution. They should be able to operate as independent contractors and choose which distributors or platforms they partner with to commodify their work, rather than being controlled by intermediaries who extract value without accountability.

At the same time, society must recognize that many patrons have unhealthy or compulsive relationships with sex. Just as programs like Gamblers Anonymous exist to address behavioral harm, resources should be available to help individuals develop healthier, more integrated relationships with intimacy. Programs should also exist to help men move away from purely transactional relationships—both those that promise sex upfront and those that offer the hope of sex later—toward relationships rooted in mutual respect and emotional connection.

Transactional relationships should not be criminalized, but neither should they be glamorized. Many men lose significant emotional, financial, and relational capital in transactional dynamics that never lead to stable, loving partnerships. Mature Masculinity calls for moving beyond the illusion of possibility toward intentional growth, responsibility, and self-development.

There is also a legitimate need for supportive, structured services that help individuals build relational skills. We do not acquire the tools for healthy adult relationships overnight. Some people require coaching, guidance, and education to form meaningful partnerships. When offered within ethical, supervised, and humanistic frameworks, such services can play a constructive role. There is evidence suggesting that legal, regulated sex work is associated with reductions in certain sex crimes, though this claim requires careful citation and contextual analysis. On the website www.decriminalizesex.work they share a list of evidence based studies that show that the decriminalization of sex work can help reduce risk and harm to the communities where decriminalization efforts took place. [167]

Ultimately, the goal is not to erase complexity but to confront it honestly—protecting the vulnerable, honoring autonomy, and building systems that reflect our highest values rather than our deepest fears.[168]

Relationships

As mentioned earlier there are countless numbers of books written about relationships. A relationship based in Mature Masculinity involves two parties that have discussed their relationship - goals, values, consent, and future building; both parties are emotionally available to give and receive of each other. There is always more to learn about your potential partner. Open and frank discussions and checking in is required. Open and frank discussions are the type that you can have once you have learned how to forgive yourself and embrace who you are or were at one point in time. I have always believed in asking my partner every few weeks or so how things are going. Is she receiving what she needs to feel loved and cared for? Is there more I can do to meet your needs? What feedback do you have for me? Early in the relationship, even during the course of dating, you should ask each other how you like to receive information and feedback. These check-ins are moments when you can address questions about when feedback could have been given earlier or at a more appropriate time. Nothing should simmer, it may take some time to bring up a situation, and if time is needed let your partner know and give them a set time of when you will respond. This allows them the opportunity to also come to terms with their feelings.

The death of most relationships is when an unresolved issue brings about contempt. Contempt is a very ugly bed fellow and is very difficult to eliminate even with counseling and virtually impossible without. Couples counseling should be introduced early into the relationship to help give a bird's eye view of the relationship. Sometimes we are too close to the relationship to see a full view of where you are and what roadblocks could hinder you from where you want to be in your relationship. In the times I have ventured into couples counseling I found that there were pockets of self-growth that I needed, as well as times where I learned that I needed to be open to my partner. Over time I have incorporated counseling techniques into my relationships and learned that sometimes it may not be you. Your partner may have a path they need to travel without you. Trust your instincts. Talk about your feelings and if you do not feel that your concerns can be resolved, then move on. Remember they are also human and deserve care, respect and kindness. They may find it hard to move on, do what you need to do to protect your mental and physical well-being.

Immature Masculinity is believing that your partner has a responsibility to do everything for you and be everything for you. You are not, nor should you be everything for your partner. Everyone has a role to play and we each play our roles. Jealousy is a natural human emotion. It is ok to feel jealous. I have felt jealous in a few relationships because I was insecure about whether or not I was good enough for her. That was my insecurity. I would speak with my partner about it, but I was not able to shake the feeling. I didn't realize that I had unresolved issues that I needed to work through. I was able to resolve these feelings during therapy. As I became more mature in my understanding of relationships and myself, I began to understand how these unresolved issues influenced my life and decisions. At the time I did not know what I was experiencing until I read books about the human experience. I learned that our experiences, the way we see the world, are filtered by our biases and the only way to truly see how we fit in the world, we need to understand and acknowledge our biases.

A relationship is a tight web of feelings, consent, openness, vulnerability, and respect between a person or group of people, conditions of which are known only to the parties involved. It is important to understand that Mature Masculinity seeks to ensure that each member of the party is satisfied and at peace. Each partner understands that each day brings different challenges and joys. True partners are able to consistently communicate their needs, wants, and desires as well as take in feedback. Taking in feedback means receiving the information from your partner and pursue ways to change the behavior, only if the request does not take away from your identity or agency. The partners are also responsible for ensuring that they give the same attention to each other as they want to be given to their needs, wants and desires. Constant communication is required. Maturity is learning how to speak and when to speak. When you do not know how to do something, true maturity is in asking for help. We do not know what we do not know and it goes doubly true when it comes to what we believe we understand about other people. For a relationship to work, silence, brooding, and hopes of mind reading abilities make only for immaturity and frustration. Frustration leads to demoralization, which leads to contempt and the cycle repeats. Being honest about your wants and expectations can help prevent the wandering eye, however we cannot stop people from wanting more. If you are not fulfilled in your relationship, have a conversation and discuss what you need and what you want to be better. If you chose to date a person that is communicative and open then it should not be difficult. If you choose the opposite then you will find yourself trying to break down an existing wall or one that you may have helped build.

This is why dating with intention is important. When you are ready and you know what you want, you can more easily and more comfortably decline relationships that do not align with your current level of maturity. If you feel that the relationship will not work, then take the time to address this with your partner with human understanding and compassion. I admit that I have been on the receiving and giving end of this. Some years ago, I had decided to date one woman exclusively, and decided to tell the other woman I was speaking to at the time. It is more common for people to date more than one person at the time. It is best to always let a potential partner know if you are dating others. When it came time to let her know of my decision, I was cold and aloof. She wanted more information from me to understand my reasoning. We had some nice moments together. The reality was I was having more fun with the other woman. I was immature in my analysis of the relationship and situation; I had not started counseling and was not ready for a mature relationship. With the other woman I had a whirlwind romance that swept me up off my feet. I didn't ask her the long list of questions I typically ask a date. All I saw was a good time, good food, and good drinks. In both cases I did not see the person, I didn't acknowledge their humanity in those moments. For that I am sorry. We all have taken the wrong turn or have been less than what we expect of ourselves. It is important that we take those pieces and use them to enhance the person we continually evolve into. We should always strive to do and be better. That is all we can ask of ourselves and our partners; be honest with yourself, be humane, be human.

Education

When I was younger and played handball at the parks in Brooklyn, I would get upset with myself if I lost a match and did not learn something from it. If I lost to someone because of my own inability to correct my game, then the loss was my own. If I lost to someone who played in ways that made me play the mental as well as the physical game, then that, to me, was an acceptable loss and one that I would study and learn from. I wanted to become a better player, possibly the best at my court and maybe the city. I played in Sunset Park, Lincoln Terrace, 2nd Ave, Coney Island, DUMBO, Chinatown, to name a few. Each place I played I learned about the court and the players. The court at Sunset Park was pitched to one side, so the ball always rolled on a slant. You could take advantage of that if you served low. At Chinatown the ball came off the wall slower and sounded different when it hit the wall. In Coney Island you would compete against paddle ball players, small ball players, the top 10 in the city, people from all around. Lincoln Terrace was home to some of the best player in Brooklyn, probably the city, and when the ball hit the wall it came off like a bullet. We were also able to play chess there and I even met a dog that thought it was a cat. In all of these experiences I learned valuable lessons. In every interaction I have is an opportunity to learn something new.

As I write this at my local bar, I heard a patron ask for an "Irish Car Bomb." I had learned that this was an offensive term to Irish people during my trip to Ireland and have never used the term since. Mature Masculinity embraces education and knowledge. Mature Masculinity understands that every experience is an opportunity to learn and become better. Understanding that we do not, and cannot, know everything is the path to true education.

Immature Masculinity sees money and sex as the end goals to our existence. Mature Masculinity understands and realizes that knowledge, understanding, and oneness in humanity are part of the true goals in this life. The school systems that are purported to dispense knowledge do a disservice to many by not explaining how each lesson affects the past, present, and future of humanity. IN many situations, students are not taught how the subject matter connects to our past and where it will take us in the future. When a student learns $a^2 + b^2 = c^2$ the full history of this concept is not always explained or understood, by both teacher and student. If adults disappeared today and only our children survived, how much of human history and progress would survive? When students learn trigonometry, they are also learning logic and postulates and how mathematical concepts are formed, intertwined and built upon each other. Mathematics is a human invention to help describe and understand the world around us, based on the observation of nature. All of the natural sciences were originally considered part of philosophy, which is why a PHD is called a Doctor of Philosophy.

Education is the path to preserving human history and providing the tools to add to it. Each conversation leads to a new idea, a new understanding, either in the person receiving the information or the person speaking. Education benefits the teacher and the student. Each connection to a thought fires off like a chain reaction creating new ideas and deeper thoughts and conversations. Have you ever experienced having a conversation with someone and a new idea popped into your head, but before it could develop and take shape, it disappeared? This happens to everyone and it is a benefit to humanity when we are able to hold on to or record that thought. We are all tasked with securing and furthering the total knowledge of humanity; this is not conveyed to us while sitting in class. We worry about a test, a forgotten homework assignment, or who likes who. We are worried about our individual lives.

This is natural. No one has the right to shame us for being human. We can hold two thoughts in our heads at the same time. We can be who we are in the moment and understand the importance of the moment. Immature Masculinity dismisses the connection we have to human history. This is not their fault. Our society has not bestowed upon teachers the proper respect and value that aligns with their value to society. They are the stalwarts and protectors of human history and human knowledge. Everything that humanity has achieved lies in the curriculum of these guardians. That is the lens that we should see educators with. This is the lens we should teach future generations to see educators with.

Once the true value of an education, and the understanding of its importance to human history, is established, society will make the necessary changes to help improve education to all. These changes are probable as more and more voices are added to the call for access to free universal education. Mature Masculinity understands the importance of every lesson and every interaction; it both cherishes and takes them to heart. In Mature Masculinity we understand that we may not be able to meet our potential in all educational settings, however we seek to find the best setting that optimizes our learning potential. Each and every one of us are protectors of human knowledge and history. We each have a part to play in securing and adding to humanity's knowledge; therefore it is important that each of us sees ourselves as protectors of the greatest aspects of humanity. There should be no shame or stigma attached to seeking an education. Education should be freely given and offered. It must be stressed, education is the cumulative work of human history, we are protecting ourselves and human history through education and in being educated. No one person, party or group should be able to control who has access to education nor the quality of education received. This should be reflected in how we treat our educators, parents, students, and the ease of access to high quality education

Protection

It is my belief that the relationship between value and protection is on an exponential scale. The more valuable, the more we are willing to protect it and the more riskier the manner in which to protect it. It is not a relationship measured in the multiple but in the exponential since the highest value is that of life. The value of life is immeasurable, and with each act of protection, the value is inversely the same. In our society there is a value to humanity, down to the penny. Each government has a dollar value assigned to a life. To a parent that has lost a child to gun violence, there is no value that justifies the loss. The life of a child is irreproachable when it comes to the value of a life. To some the value of a life prebirth is valued the same as a life after birth. What values do we decide to protect? Who do we decide to protect? It is not a simple question nor solution. The value of protection works in conjunction with what society and humanity deems worthy. Dying for a cause is considered the greatest of sacrifices. How do you evaluate the worth of a life that died fighting for Germany and the other for the US during World War II? Your evaluation, of the value of each life, depends on the cause of each country. If the cause changes the value changes. It is society that dictates value which are then reflected in the Overton Window of that time period. Freedom of speech is valued highly in America, pending what you are allowed to say, and who is doing the speaking. The scale of that value is the Overton Window. As an value moves further away from societal acceptance, the need to protect the value also changes.

If freedom of speech is agreed to be "highly important" by 70% of Americans and is on the upper end of the Overton Window then the value of one's life in the protection of "freedom of speech" is valued accordingly. If a woman's right to choose has 70% approval but is not highly valued by society, as measured through the Overton Window, then it is a position not worth the ultimate sacrifice of life. In Mature Masculinity the value is not based on the current Overton Window, but on the effect on humanity. Does the concept further the advancement of humanity and protect the future of humanity. A person's right to bear a child is a personal right borne by those able to bear children. Those of us unable to bear children have no rights in the final decision because the process does not directly impact our immediate wellbeing. We may be affected by their decision later and this will require time, patience, communication, and understanding to heal - on both sides. Each side requires empathy and sympathy from the other as well as direct communication and counseling. In Mature Masculinity if we, as men, better ourselves we will be better partners, better parents, and have better relationships; and ultimately be better protectors. All choices should be made from a place of protection and in a frame of mind that consists of love, care and support. Many today do not have these protections, therefore the protection of the freedom to choose is paramount. I only use this as an example of how ideas can compromise the values we put on ourselves and humanity.

Mature Masculinity encompasses the belief that we protect humanity and the ability to make our own choices. Every choice we make, whether good or bad, advances humanity; we learn from our mistakes and take pride in our advancements. Humanity is not only the people, but also our society, with the principles of Mature Masculinity protecting both. Every choice should be made with a human connection in mind and a place in our collective history. Who we are is a product of evolution - our hopes, humanity's acquired knowledge, the quest to find a sense of self as well as our place in the universe. Every person has a story to tell, and every person should have a safe place to tell it. In each notch in our shared history, we have always been a singular race of people. Whether black, white, Asian, hetero, bi, gay straight, trans, cis male, cis female, queer, we have always been. We all exist. We are the dust of the cosmos made flesh. This is what we protect. We continue to get lost in the forest of "Other" and forget about "We." The concept of "We" is protected in humanity, because "We" is the concept of a people. I write "a people," to identify the all-encompassing humanity as an identifier. All are the protectors of humanity. Mature Masculinity understands and sees its place at the wall protecting it all - what we say, what we do, how we speak and how we improve. Humanity is not static; we evolve and become better. We protect in our strength, which is tied ultimately to humanity's fate. This sounds fatalistic and grand, but it is how I see each individual and the impact we can have.

I would be remiss by not speaking about another type of protection that Mature Masculinity is charged with – Science and Critical Thinking. Science lives in the mind and consciousness of the Mature Masculine man.

Critical thinking and humility are the armor worn by those that choose to be protectors of humanity. Some seek understanding and help through the invisible hand of God. Some believe that their fate is paved by their own hands. Some question "If we have free will, do we have the will to attribute our actions to our own hand and not that of the divine?" We would protect ourselves and our society more if we acknowledge the role we play in human history. It is not to say the divine does not exist or exists, it's about acknowledging and accepting our role in humanity's survival and doing all we can to protect us. What happens will happen, we can only protect today, and plan for tomorrow. This requires critical thinking, knowledge of the scientific process, a strong sense of empathy and humanity, and humility. These are foundational to Mature Masculinity.

Resilience, Hard Work, and Effort

The world is a hard place to navigate. Every day we make choices that can make our lives easier or more difficult. Mature Masculinity is a concept that requires hard work and effort to implement. It also requires a great deal of resilience. As we redefine masculinity, there will be pushback as to how we conduct ourselves and the expectations we have for ourselves and others. In everything we do we must always consider our impact on humanity. No matter how small we believe we are in the grand scheme, we play a part in the Butterfly Effect. Each time a person observes your efforts at redefining masculinity, they are affected. It may become a story they tell their friends and family or something they keep in the back of their minds. Each effort builds towards greater change, collective change, societal change. Changing a mentality that has been force unto us will require hard work and a great deal of effort from all areas of society. As we build up the foundation and framework of Mature Masculinity and redefine masculinity, we must also be resilient by not slipping back into the previous way of Immature Masculinity; but if we do, we must be willing to forgive ourselves and strive to do better.

This takes hard work and effort on the part of every individual and group that wants to see masculinity redefined for the greater good of humanity. It is a burdensome task, which is why each of us must do our part. Fellowship and support of men is required, from everyone, in every walk of life. Removing stigmas surrounding mental health and masculinity is required. We cannot build anew if the old is not torn down. Every effort a man makes to better himself and the world around him, should be acknowledged for the good and positive impacts they create - for themselves, their communities, and society. Each act of maturity should be shouted out from the mountain top, to let those who are struggling know that there is a mountain top and it can be climbed. We can all get there, with hard work, resilience, and a great deal of effort - never alone, always together…. always forward.

Compassion over Violence

As men we are taught to be strong and to not be compromised by anyone. We are the kings of the world, the law makers, we hold dominion and govern over all. If our rule is threatened by anyone, we attack. We are prone to fight before flight. If our masculinity is threatened we may commit acts of violence or aggression that may be outside of our normal character. Some chalk it to the testosterone flowing in our veins. When men are hitting puberty we are at that sweet spot of unbridled testosterone and an undeveloped prefrontal cortex. We do stupid things. It is said we are horny all the time, emotional, all while looking to find our place in the world. That can be a dangerous combination, especially when you throw in peer pressure. How many videos have we seen of young boys and men doing dangerous stunts or resorting to violence to make themselves feel manly or get attention? This is toxic and Immature Masculinity at its finest.

How does one choose compassion over violence if one is not taught how to be compassionate? As humans we are storytellers. We tell stories to relay a message, but to also feel important. When one tells a story, all eyes are on them. Every word, every breath, each intonation is absorbed and as a listener, we become part of the story. Violence makes a story more interesting, we sometimes find ourselves instigating a conflict to have a story to tell, it is human nature, but not human nurture. Empathy and compassion are two traits that society does not do a great job at promoting in men. There are organizations that promote both but get washed away in the "me" or self-absorption of society. Mature Masculinity deals in conflict resolution, compassion and empathy. Proper conflict resolution moves along this conversation path: We need to first understand the problem. Talk it out. Tell me what your problem is and I will repeat what you said back to you in my own words to make sure I understand. Listen to me and tell me what you believe I am saying. Once you understand each other's position, try to put yourself in their shoes. Try to understand why they feel the way they do. Is there a misunderstanding? Was something lost in translation? Did one of us make an assumption? These are conflict resolution techniques similar to Collaborative Conflict Resolution, Perspective Taking, Non Violent Communication, and F.L.A.M.E (Find Out, Listen, Analyze, Mediate, Explain).[169]

Once you have found empathy or understanding, find a resolution that deals in compassion. If you need to walk away, try to do so with some goal of future resolution or be resolved that there may be no solution. Not all situations can be resolved immediately. Some resolutions take time. Be compassionate when working through the issue. Anger makes us defensive. We push out to protect ourselves from harm. Bruce Lee is quoted as saying "Be like water making its way through cracks. Do not be assertive, but adjust to the object, and you shall find a way around or through it. If nothing within you stays rigid, outward things will disclose themselves. Empty your mind, be formless. Shapeless, like water. If you put water into a cup, it becomes the cup. You put water into a bottle and it becomes the bottle. You put it in a teapot, it becomes the teapot. Now, water can flow or it can crash. Be water, my friend."[170] Find ways to be fluid in your handling of a conflict. There are many options available to us to find peace of mind and one's soul in a conflict. Be open to reading books about conflict resolution, which will give you more tools to help strengthen your compassion, empathy, self-reflectivity and thoughtfulness when faced with conflicts in your daily life. Knowledge is the key to obtaining true peace.

Conflict resolution, empathy and compassion are traits that should be taught at home and in everyday society. These are traits that are at the apex of the good in humanity. Immature Masculinity cares only for power, regardless of who is hurt by it. Immature Masculinity cannot walk away from a fight or an insult. Immature Masculinity does not take time to understand the other. This problem lies bare at the feet of our society. We continue to send men out to war for conflicts they never started or for causes they have no care for. What compassion do we teach them when we withhold funds to provide medical aid, food and shelter? We don't teach compassion, we teach "me." We assume that boys will grow up and mature and leave behind their impulses toward violence. How can they!? When they are reminded every day, through the pain and suffering consuming our world, that their bodies are made for war. We have to be better. We have to do better. Our path toward change is similar to a disc placed in the game Othello. Each strategic placement of our compassion and empathy, used to resolve conflict, affects the observer and participants and extends the influence of these traits. This is how we heal humanity and each other, by choosing compassion over violence.

Chapter Summary

This Chapter lays out the difference between Immature Masculinity, the script society hands to boys without caring about their humanity; and Mature Masculinity, which requires self-reflection, empathy, responsibility, and the courage to grow. We discussed what toxic masculinity actually is, how it comes from social pressures placed on men, and why the better term for many of these behaviors is Immature Masculinity rather than toxic masculinity. From construction sites to dating, conflict, sex, consent, and fatherhood, we explore how men are shaped, how we harm ourselves and others, and how maturity requires honesty, intention, and respect.

This chapter also wrestles with the deeper responsibilities tied to masculinity - protecting humanity, embracing education, rejecting violence as the first language, and choosing compassion even when ego demands the opposite. It challenges men to understand their role in sexuality, the law of consequences, consent, trauma, accountability, and how power dynamics shape behavior. Most importantly, it makes clear that Mature Masculinity is not a destination; it is a discipline. It is the willingness to confront who we are, learn from our failures, and build something better—for ourselves, our partners, our children, and humanity as a whole.

Main Points

- Immature Masculinity is the inherited script, rooted in power, ego, and unexamined pain while Mature Masculinity is a conscious choice rooted in empathy, self-reflection, accountability, and humanity.

- Mature Masculinity asks men to confront their own trauma, understand consent and power, build healthy relationships, honor their role in sexuality and reproduction, and reject societal expectations that deny men their humanity.

- The path to Mature Masculinity is ongoing work including education, resilience, compassion over violence, fellowship with other men, and a commitment to protecting humanity, not dominating it.

Chapter 8

F.E.A.R - Forgiveness, Empathy, Accountability, Redemption

I strongly believe that the number one issue in our world is the inability to allow for redemption. There is no clear path for redemption in our society, you are either with or against us, bad or good, right or wrong. We now live in a world where right can be wrong and wrong can be right, depending on where you received your information. If I am told that I am wrong by someone with a different value system from my own, I am less likely to believe them. We are more willing to push further in our wrongness than to admit or give thought to the possibility that we may be wrong. If we are wrong, then it feels as though the whole world knows we are wrong and we face the fear of being ridiculed. This fear leaves no room for redemption. Forgiveness, Empathy, Accountability, and Redemption or F.E.A.R are part of a cycle of renewal and strength that we need to embrace more in society, starting with men.

Empathy is the first path to the cycle of renewal and strength that is found in Mature Masculinity. I have stressed throughout this book the importance of empathy. It is truly the only path forward, because it connects us to the root of our humanity - our feelings and emotions. When we are able to stand in someone else's pain, joy, sadness, or anger, we become a part of them. We can be there for them in their moments of vulnerability and share the burden, lessening their load, all while enhancing the human connectivity between two people. Time and time again studies show the benefit of social interaction and empathy during times of need and friendships. The metadata study "Adult friendship and wellbeing: A systematic review with practical implications" gives insight into the overall positive effect friendships can have "A total of 38 research articles published between 2000 and 2019 were reviewed. In general, adult friendship was found to predict or at least be positively correlated with wellbeing and its components. In particular, the results showed that friendship quality and socializing with friends predict wellbeing levels. In addition, number of friends, their reactions to their friend's attempts of capitalizing positive events, support of friend's autonomy, and efforts to maintain friendship are positively correlated with wellbeing."[171] Through empathy we strengthen our relationships, which is what we strive for in Mature Masculinity. This same empathy muscle is used when we also try to resolve conflict, as noted in the last chapter. This is where empathy leads to accountability.

When we understand how we have harmed someone or offended them, we should then hold ourselves accountable for the pain caused and the breach in the relationship. Accountability is not only acknowledging the misstep, but also taking ownership of what led to the breach, the results, and why you need to acknowledge the responsibility. There is fear in taking accountability. The fear is in the outcome after you have taken responsibility, when the next resolution is not in your control. It is easier to breathe a sigh of relief once you are in hindsight, but it's harder to live through it and even harder to let go. It is important that during the transition from taking accountability and being held accountable, that we find some way towards peace. Stress can cause anxiety and cause you to further hurt others. Try to be present in the moment and push through to the other side. As a project manager I am very familiar with both sides of this spectrum. I hold myself and the contractors I work with accountability for every success and every failure. I work with them through the issues to find resolution. The anxiety before reaching a deal or solution keeps me up at night, but the calm after helps me sleep. Try to discover different coping mechanisms to help you through the anxious moments. I tend to do a lot of reflection on what I could have done better and how I can apply that the next time. I also tend to not eat when I am anxious, and I love to eat. Finding your own way to peace during these anxious moments is important as is self-reflection. These will allow you to be accountable while helping to make you a better person. Accountability is the first part of the path to forgiveness, forgiveness of yourself and of others.

The hardest test of forgiveness for me, was when I had to forgive God. He took away one of the most important people in my life. I pleaded, I begged, I visited her every day in the hospital. I wanted my grandmother back. I still want her back. I realized that part of the reason why I needed her so much was partly because I didn't think I was ready for a world without her. She had always been my foundation and my rock. How can I be that for my daughter if mine is no longer here? I began to realize that my anger was more at myself, wondering if I could do more. In order to find a path to peace, I had to find a way to forgive God. I still had my daughter and I had to change my point of view to see the positive and not the negative. I was still alive. I am a testament to who she was, her impact, and what she meant to humanity. I find it humbling that we received a letter from President Jimmy Carter and First Lady Roslyn Carter after her passing. With the passing of the Carters, it means all the more to my family and I hope this book is a way to pay our respect to the Carters and their legacy.

It took time and therapy to get to a place where I no longer blamed God and have eventually forgiven God. I think often of that reflection point, where I found myself on both ends of the forgiveness spectrum. The hardest form of forgiveness is forgiving yourself. Some are able to forgive the world and are not willing to forgive themselves for being human. We are all fallible and we do our best in the capacity we can. When we are unable to forgive ourselves, we take away from our potential. We weigh ourselves down with the burden of guilt and shame. We cannot begin to heal because we are unable to forgive ourselves, and the wound remains open. Mature Masculinity allows us to forgive ourselves and others. There are times when one may not be able to find the capacity for forgiveness, even in those times we should try to forgive ourselves for not being able to forgive. There are some traumatic experiences that can cause irreparable damage that even therapy may not be able to fix. If you cannot forgive the other, forgive yourself and find a way to be at peace. When you are finally at peace, think again about forgiveness, and if you are still unable to forgive, be in your peace. Being able to forgive is hard. It is not immature to not be able to forgive, it is immature to take out your frustrations and pain on others, even the person that has caused you pain. There is justice in this world and we need to allow it to play out. Concentrate on healing and becoming a better, more mature person. All roads lead to redemption.

We can forgive, we can empathize, and we can hold each other accountable, but what about redemption. What is the path forward towards redemption? How does one redeem themselves in the eyes of society, in the eyes of the community, in the eyes of those that love you? Redemption is a difficult path. It is a path that many religions speak of. I have observed this most closely in the Christian community. In Christianity all are sinners and have fallen short of the glory of God. We can only be saved by accepting Jesus Christ into our hearts. Christianity has redemption sown into its culture. Christianity is built on the understanding that people are sinful by nature and that only through Jesus can we find redemption. Redemption is something that only God can give. If someone asks for forgiveness, in their hearts, and is saved, then who are we to judge them? God knows their hearts and mind and Christians respect this interpersonal relationship. I hypothesize that this is why it is easier for a leader in the Christian ranks, and/or Christian, communities to make a mistake, be forgiven and find redemption in the Church. I am using Christianity as an example since it is a concept I am more familiar with having grown up in the Christian Church.

During the pandemic I had the opportunity to learn about the concepts of "Restorative Justice" and "Restorative Practices" a vehicles for redemption. Their definitions are as follows:

- "Restorative Justice - is an approach to justice that aims to repair the harm done to victims. In doing so, practitioners work to ensure that offenders take responsibility for their actions, to understand the harm they have caused, to give them an opportunity to redeem themselves, and to discourage them from causing further harm.

For victims, the goal is to give them an active role in the process, and to reduce feelings of anxiety and powerlessness."[172]

- "Restorative Practice - Restorative practices is a social science that studies how to improve and repair relationships between people and communities. The purpose is to build healthy communities, increase social capital, decrease crime and antisocial behavior, repair harm and restore relationships. It ties together research in a variety of social science fields, including education, psychology, social work, criminology, sociology, organizational development and leadership. Restorative practices are a tool that have been growing in popularity since the early 2000s, but researchers still struggle to define restorative practices (or RP) as a whole."[173]

Restorative Justice and Restorative Practices are ways in which humanity can find the paths forward to healing and reconciling with individuals and groups of people. The biggest hurdle to redemption is ego. Even though humans are great at adapting to change, we are most reluctant to change, because of fear of the unknown. We know that we can change our behavior and improve our lives through these changes, but our ego prevents us from changing. Change requires hard work and continual effort and sometimes our minds are locked into who we are today, so that we cannot see who we can become tomorrow. Restorative practices and restorative justice are paths that lead to redemption for all who truly engage with the process and seek redemption. Mature Masculinity seeks out a path forward for all of humanity and advocates the use of any practice that leads to a path of redemption, to allow for healing and the advancement of humanity.

Religion has redemption built into its world view. This is why many prisoners turn to religion when they are incarcerated. In a world where restorative justice is in its infancy, the only path, in a prisoner's mind, is redemption is through religion. We need to change this model and make it available in our everyday lives.

Forgiveness, Empathy, Accountability, Redemption are some of the core concepts that will allow humanity to continue forward. In this new definition of Masculinity, the terms "Immature Masculinity" and "Mature Masculinity" can come off as divisive and separationist. As I stated at the beginning, I have immature masculine tendencies. I am part of that element, but I am working on myself. I am in the loop of continual improvement or Kaizen. I had to learn and understand what empathy truly meant and how to engage with people through empathy. I had to learn how to forgive myself and others, which I was able to accomplish with therapy and self-reflection. I try to hold myself accountable for my actions and seek forgiveness when I have wronged another, knowingly or unknowingly and always a work in progress. As I have learned to seek forgiveness, I also try to learn to forgive others. The more hurt I am by the person, the harder it has been to forgive, and when I do come to a point where I can find forgiveness in my heart, I have found that the healing continues in me. All paths lead to redemption. This is the part where society and individuals have the most difficulty. If the concept of redemption is integrated into our everyday lives and we see how the arc of redemption works, we would be more willing to open our hearts and acknowledge that people can change for the better.

Chapter Summary

In this chapter we explored why forgiveness, empathy, accountability, and redemption are central to Mature Masculinity and to the healing of our wider society. We looked at how fear and ego block us from growth, why empathy strengthens our relationships, and how accountability requires accepting responsibility even when the outcome is uncertain. I shared my own challenges with forgiveness to show how difficult but necessary that work can be, especially when we need to forgive ourselves. We also reviewed restorative justice and restorative practices as real pathways toward repair and renewal. The goal of this chapter was to show that redemption is possible, but only when we engage with these four principles with honesty and intention.

Main Points

- Redemption is missing from our culture, and without a real path back, people stay stuck in fear, denial, and performance instead of growth.

- Forgiveness, empathy, accountability, and redemption (F.E.A.R) are not abstract virtues but practical skills that men must learn, practice, and model if we want Mature Masculinity to mean anything.

- Restorative justice and restorative practices give us a concrete framework for redemption, but ego and fear of change are the main enemies we have to face in ourselves and in our systems.

Chapter 9
Conclusion

We are at the end of this long journey in discovering what Mature and Immature Masculinity are and what a world of Mature Masculinity could look like.

It was always my intention to begin this book with critical thinking because that was the beginning of my own journey. When I was younger, I often found myself arguing with friends about my beliefs without tangible evidence or a solid foundation beneath them. When they questioned my logic, I believed I was responding with wit and knowledge. A friend once gave me a book on logical fallacies and fallacious arguments. I did not read it, because I thought I already knew better.As I began my journey into management, my beliefs about what a good manager should and should not do were challenged. I was introduced to Dale Carnegie and How to Win Friends and Influence People. I started listening to podcasts about history, science, psychology, and the human experience. I realized that I had always been interested in everything, yet I did not understand how little I truly knew. That realization pushed me toward logic and mathematical proofs—not only because I wanted to win arguments, but also because I had spent so much of my life wanting to be right. Critical thinking taught me something far more valuable than correctness: humility.

I started this book by discussing the importance of critical thinking, and I have challenged the reader not merely to absorb information, but to engage with it—to research further, question assumptions, and examine evidence independently. This book is part of a larger and ongoing conversation that has accelerated in this century. That conversation requires open hearts and open minds, along with tools that help us navigate disinformation and misinformation. Every small group circulates information to strengthen internal bonds under a single banner. The rallying cry becomes, "There is no outside information—only what we tell you."

You have the choice to step back, to learn more, and to question the writer, the premise given, and the information provided. You have the right to seek alternate sources. When a group denies or limits access to information, that is when the first cracks appear. Critical thinking requires that an argument hold up under scrutiny and be grounded in evidence. Given the controversial nature of this discussion, it is essential to begin from a place of facts and evidence, while understanding that correlation is not causation. A deeper understanding of both allows us to interpret data more accurately and make better decisions.

Humanity—not masculinity—is the overarching theme of this book. Humanity is the history upon which masculinity was built. Humanity breathed life into masculinity in the same way it birthed hunter-gatherer societies, egalitarianism, the Stone Age, the Bronze Age, agriculture, construction, art, science, mathematics, steam engines, technology, artificial intelligence, and beyond. Each stage of history reflects how basic survival needs evolve during times of surplus. When those needs are met, the biological drive to reproduce and continue genetic lineage persists. With surplus comes the ability to support more offspring, and with more offspring comes increased demand for resources. Throughout history, the decision to take another group's resources has often been justified in the name of survival. Scientific data shows that men have historically been shaped into the primary instruments of war. History also shows how men have been used to acquire land and resources for those in power, often living off the remnants of those gains.

For centuries, societies have imposed tests and requirements that boys must meet to be recognized as men. Each culture developed its own definition of manhood. In modern times, the Bem Sex Role Inventory attempted to catalog socially accepted masculine and feminine traits in Western society. Masculinity has never been defined solely by biology. Traits such as leadership, decisiveness, conviction, and action became associated with men. Over time, additional expectations were layered on: emotional stoicism, physical strength, resilience without complaint, unwavering endurance. Men are surrounded by symbols reinforcing these ideals—trucks, guns, military imagery, alcohol, sexual conquest, sacrifice, danger, excess, relentless labor. These pressures have contributed to what Dr. Warren Farrell termed the modern "Boy Crisis."

As society has made necessary—though overdue—course corrections to advance women's inclusion in education and professional fields such as STEAM, the education system reveals another reality: boys and men are increasingly falling behind. Some attribute this to differences in maturation rates; others propose structural changes such as same-sex education. At present, the evidence does not conclusively support these solutions. What the data does show is a need for deeper study into executive function, emotional development, and educational support tailored to boys. A "Purpose Void" has emerged one where modern expectations of masculinity no longer align with the realities boys and men face.

I am reminded of the words of a woman speaking about Black men during an interview surrounding the Biden–Trump election rematch in November 2023. She noted that society had propped up a gendered lie that men would naturally rise and benefit from systemic advantage yet that promise has not materialized for Black men. This has created a profound question of identity and purpose.[174] Black men are disproportionately affected by the Boy Crisis and the Purpose Void, though all men have felt their impact to varying degrees. Boys and men have increasingly become an afterthought. Addressing education, fatherhood, and mental health does not diminish the progress made by women. It is a call to recognize unintended consequences and restore balance.

Education is the foundation of understanding. Intellectual and emotional education expands horizons. If you spend your life staring at a wall, you cannot see the city behind it. Even once past the wall, if you cannot elevate yourself, you will never see how everything connects. Education offers a path beyond rigid social definitions of masculinity. As comedian Christopher Titus often says, "Education is a national security issue."[175] Fatherhood extends beyond raising children; it includes mentorship and modeling healthy masculinity. The same way burdens are passed down, healing can be passed forward.

Fellowship and camaraderie allow positive examples of masculinity and humanity to spread. Pride can exist without diminishing women. We are all part of humanity, and progress depends on cooperation. Mental health and self-care challenge traditional masculine norms, yet remain essential. Access remains a barrier. Healthcare—physical and mental— should be recognized as a human right. Many challenges are genetic or environmental, yet our humanity is measured by our willingness to support one another. This is the scale upon which mature and Immature Masculinity are weighed.

Respect for others and oneself; bodily autonomy; enthusiastic consent; dating with intention and honesty; understanding the gravity of sexual relationships; valuing connection and future consequence; protecting education, creativity, and human dignity—these are traits of Mature Masculinity. Mature Masculinity says "we", not "me." Immature Masculinity sees only the self, often disguising exploitation as brotherhood or justice. It rejects accountability, dismisses mental health care, dehumanizes outsiders, and demands obedience in exchange for protection. This is masculinity divorced from humanity.

Masculinity itself is neither good nor bad. It is a collection of traits attributed to male behavioral patterns. No man choses the burden of masculinity; it was assigned through family, culture, and history. Words, however, are not fixed. Their meanings evolve. Men can redefine masculinity—or abandon the term altogether in favor of humanity. We can reject inherited definitions and choose a better path. We are not alone. We exist within a continuum across time, each of us a concept capable of shaping the world.

As humans, we are custodians of humanity for those who follow. This can be achieved through F.E.A.R.: Forgiveness, Empathy, Accountability, and Redemption.

How will you take a stand today—changing your world, your perspective, your life—one step at a time?

Appendix A
List of Therapy Groups for Men

North America

1. **RAINN** (U.S.)

   o   Offers a 24/7 confidential hotline and chat for survivors of sexual violence, regardless of gender. RAINN+1

2. **1 in 6** (U.S.)

   o   Focused on men who have experienced sexual abuse or assault. Free resources, online groups, helpline. 1in6.org

3. **MaleSurvivor** (U.S. / online)

   o   Dedicated to men sexually abused or assaulted (childhood or adult). Offers moderated forums, chats, peer groups. MaleSurvivor

4. **Boston Area Rape Crisis Center (BARCC)** (U.S.)

   o   Has programs for male survivors including group and individual counselling. BARCC

5. **National Sexual Violence Resource Center (NSVRC)** (U.S.)

   o   Provides research, tools for advocates, and has specific material on "Working with Male Survivors of Sexual Violence". NSVRC+1

Global / International

1. **All Survivors Project**

   o   Focuses on conflict-related sexual violence (CRSV) against men and boys worldwide. allsurvivorsproject.org

Appendix B
References

[1] Warren Farrell and John Gray, The Boy Crisis: Why Our Boys Are Struggling and What We Can Do About It (Dallas: BenBella Books, 2018).

[2] Rick Warren, The Purpose Driven Life: What on Earth Am I Here For? (Grand Rapids, MI: Zondervan, 2002), 27.

[3] Warren Farrell and John Gray, The Boy Crisis: Why Our Boys Are Struggling and What We Can Do About It (Dallas: BenBella Books, 2018).

[4] Christina Hoff Sommers, The War Against Boys: How Misguided Policies Are Harming Our Young Men, rev. ed. (New York: Simon & Schuster, 2013).

[5] Richard V. Reeves, Of Boys and Men: Why the Modern Male Is Struggling, Why It Matters, and What to Do About It (Washington, D.C.: Brookings Institution Press, 2022).

[6] Dale Carnegie, How to Win Friends and Influence People (New York: Simon and Schuster, 1936).

[7] Kahneman, Daniel, and Amos Tversky. "Judgment under Uncertainty: Heuristics and Biases." Science 185, no. 4157 (September 27, 1974): 1124–1131. https://doi.org/10.1126/science.185.4157.1124

[8] Hope Reese, "Robert Sapolsky and the End of Free Will," The New York Times, February 16, 2023

[9] Susan Blackmore and Kevin Mitchell, "Debate: Free Will is an Illusion," Intelligence Squared, podcast audio, January 24, 2024

[10] Follman, M., Aronsen, G., & Pan, D. (2023). US Mass Shootings, 1982–2023: Data from Mother Jones' Investigation. Mother Jones.

[11] Warren Farrell and John Gray, The Boy Crisis: Why Our Boys Are Struggling and What We Can Do About It (Dallas: BenBella Books, 2018)

[12] Brian J Morris, Stephen MOreton, Stefan A Baills Guy Cox, John N. Kreiger, "Critical evaluation of contrasting evidence on whether male circumcision has adverse psychological effects: A systematic review", Journal of Evidence-Based

Medicine/Volume 15, Issue 2 p. 123-135. Downloaded from Wiley Online Library https://doi.org/10.1111/jebm.12482

[13] Martie G. Haselton, Daniel Nettle, and Damian R. Murray, The Evolution of Cognitive Bias (Cambridge: Cambridge University Press, 2005).

[14] Geoff Cummings, Intro Statistics 9: The Dance of the P-value, YouTube video, 12:35, posted by "Geoff Cummings," May 3, 2017

[15] Tetlock, P. E., Ditto, J. S., & Kahan, D. M. (2011). Motivated numeracy and enlightened self-government. Behavioral Public Policy, 1(1), 10-31.

[16] Tara Swart, "The 4 Underlying Principles of Changing Your Brain," Forbes, March 27, 2018, https://www.forbes.com/sites/taraswart/2018/03/27/the-4-underlying-principles-to-changing-your-brain/.

[17] Botvinik-Nezer, R., Jones, M., & Wager, T. D. (2023). A belief systems analysis of fraud beliefs following the 2020 US election. Nature Human Behaviour, 7(9), 1446–1459. https://doi.org/10.1038/s41562-023-01650-9

[18] Novella, Steven. "The Skeptics Guide to the Universe." Podcast. Last modified [date]. https://www.theskepticsguide.org/.

[19] Dale Carnegie, How to Win Friends and Influence People (New York: Simon and Schuster, 1936), [page number if applicable].

[20] Slon, V., Mafessoni, F., Vernot, B. et al. The genome of the offspring of a Neanderthal mother and a Denisovan father. Nature 561, 113–116 (2018). https://doi.org/10.1038/s41586-018-0455-x

[21] Diamond, J. (1997). Guns, Germs, and Steel: The Fates of Human Societies. New York: W.W. Norton & Company.

[22] Harari, Y. N. (2015). Sapiens: A Brief History of Humankind. London: Harvill Secker.

[23] Vivek Vankataraman, Ancient men were hunters and women were gatherers. Right? Wrong? The Conversation March 13, 2021 at 7:30 PM. from amp.scroll.in.

[24] Brown, J. (1970). Women in Prehistory: The State of the Debate. In Sex and Gender: A Reader in Feminist Theory (pp. 158-172). Routledge.

25 Hawkes, K., O'Connell, J. F., & Blurton Jones, N. G. (1997). Hadza women's time allocation, offspring provisioning, and the evolution of human life histories. Current Anthropology, 38(4), 547-570.

26 Earle, T. (1997). How Chiefs Come to Power: The Political Economy in Prehistory. Stanford University Press.

27 Diamond, J. (1997). Guns, Germs, and Steel: The Fates of Human Societies. New York: W.W. Norton & Company.

28 Sell, A., Tooby, J., & Cosmides, L. (2009). Formidability and the logic of human anger. Proceedings of the National Academy of Sciences, 106(35), 15073-15078.

29 Sell, A., Tooby, J., & Cosmides, L. (2012). The Importance of Physical Strength to Human Males. Human Nature, 23(1), 30–44.

30 Micheletti AJC, Ruxton GD, Gardner A. Why war is a man's game. Proc Biol Sci. 2018 Aug 15;285(1884):20180975. doi: 10.1098/rspb.2018.0975. PMID: 30111597; PMCID: PMC6111185.

31 Baker, R. R., & Bellis, M. A. (1993). Human sperm competition: Ejaculate economics. Animal Behaviour, 46(3), 561-567.

32 Alves da Silva, C. S., Mafra, A. L., & Valentova, J. V. (2025). Evolutionary Role of the Female Orgasm: Insights into Mate Choice and Beyond. Archives of Sexual Behavior, 54(1), 323–334.

33 Bauch, C., McElreath, R. Disease dynamics and costly punishment can foster socially imposed monogamy. Nat Commun 7, 11219 (2016). https://doi.org/10.1038/ncomms11219

34 Silva, M. A. (2010). Women in Ancient Japan: From Matriarchal Antiquity to Acquiescent Confinement. Inquiries Journal, 2(04). Retrieved from Inquiries Journal "Chinese records dating back to the first century reveal that women were not only allowed to rule, but also encouraged to rule …"

35 Murasaki Shikibu. (1990). The tale of Genji (E. G. Seidensticker, Trans.). New York, NY: Vintage International.

36 Mallary A. Silva Women in Ancient Japan: From Matriarchal Antiquity to Acquiescent Confinement, Inquiries Journal social science, arts, and humanities 2010 vol 2 No. 09 pg 1/1

37 Wikipedia contributors. (n.d.). Creswellian culture. In Wikipedia. Retrieved August 16, 2025, from Wikipedia website.

38 Diamond, J. (2012). The World Until Yesterday: What Can We Learn from Traditional Societies? New York: Viking. p. 23.

39 Diamond, J. M. (2012). The world until yesterday: What can we learn from traditional societies? New York, NY: Viking.

40 Peterson, V. S. (2014). Sex matters. International Feminist Journal of Politics.

41 Strang, V. (2014). Lording it over the goddess: Water, gender, and human–environmental relations. Journal of Feminist Studies in Religion, 30(1), 83–107.

42 Parsons, T. (1944). The theoretical development of the sociology of religion: A chapter in the history of modern social science. Journal of the History of Ideas.

43 See generally Susan Abernethy, Anglo Saxon Women in England, Hypothesis August 8 2013

44 Office for National Statistics, Labour Market Overview, UK: February 2023, Labour Market Bulletin, Table A02.SA (14 February 2023), https://www.ons.gov.uk/employmentandlabourmarket/peopleinwork/empl oymentandemployeetypes/datasets/employmentunemploymentandeconomic inactivityforpeopleaged16andoverandagedfrom16to64seasonallyadjusteda02sa

45 See generally National Archives: America's Founding Documents - The Bill of Rights How did it happen, online searched 11/4/2023 https://www.archives.gov/founding-docs/bill-of-rights/how-did-it-happen#:~:text=A%20joint%20House%20and%20Senate,the%20%E2%80%9CBill%20of%20Rights.%E2%80%9D

46 Schlafly, P. (1977). The Power of the Positive Woman. New Rochelle, NY: Arlington House.

47 Ibid

48 Bem, S. L. (1974). The measurement of psychological androgyny. Journal of Consulting and Clinical Psychology, 42(2), 155–162. https://doi.org/10.1037/h0036215

[49] American Psychological Association. (n.d.). Bem Sex-Role Inventory (BSRI). In APA Dictionary of Psychology. Retrieved from https://dictionary.apa.org/bem-sex-role-inventory

[50] Stoet, G. (n.d.). Bem Sex Role Inventory (BSRI). PsyToolkit. Retrieved from https://www.psytoolkit.org/survey-library/bemsexrole.html

[51] Campbell, A., Gillaspy, J. A., & Thompson, B. (1997). The factor structure of the Bem Sex-Role Inventory (BSRI): Confirmatory analysis of long and short forms. Educational and Psychological Measurement, 57(1), 118–124. https://doi.org/10.1177/0013164497057001007

[52] Takala, T. (1998). Philosophy of Leadership: A Study of the Works of Plato, Aristotle, and Confucius. Journal of Leadership Studies, 5(2), 21-34.

[53] Machiavelli, N. (1513/1992). The Prince (W. K. Marriott, Trans.). New York: Dover Publications.

[54] Carlyle, T. (1841/2011). On Heroes, Hero-Worship, and the Heroic in History. New York: Dover Publications

[55] Silva, A. (2016) What Is Leadership? Journal of Business Studies Quarterly, 8, 1-5.

[56] Willink, J., & Babin, L. (2015). Extreme Ownership: How U.S. Navy SEALs Lead and Win. New York: St. Martin's Press.

[57] Carnegie, D. (1936). How to Win Friends and Influence People. New York: Simon and Schuster.

[58] Living Colour. (1988). Cult of Personality. Vivid. Epic Records.

[59] Patton, G. S. (1974). War as I Knew It. Boston: Houghton Mifflin Company.

[60] Bellamy, A. J. (n.d.). Humans may have evolved aggression, but that doesn't mean we were hard wired for war.

[61] Ferguson, B. (2013). War is Not Part of Human Nature. Scientific American, 308(6), 84-89.

[62] Maynard Smith, J. (1982). Evolution and the Theory of Games. Cambridge: Cambridge University Press.

[63] LeBlanc, S. A., & Register, K. E. (2003). Constant Battles: The Myth of the Peaceful, Noble Savage. St. Martin's Press.

[64] Mark Briffa, Sarah M. Lane, Signals in Conflict Resolution: Conventional Signals, Aggression and Territoriality, Editor(s): Jae Chun Choe, Encyclopedia of Animal Behavior (Second Edition), Academic Press,2019,Pages 531-538, ISBN 9780128132524, https://doi.org/10.1016/B978-0-12-809633-8.90701-5.

(https://www.sciencedirect.com/science/article/pii/B9780128096338907015)

[65] Wrangham, R. W. (2018). Two Types of Aggression in Human Evolution. The Quarterly Review of Biology, 93(4), 365-379.

[66] Wrangham, R. W. (2019). The Goodness Paradox: The Strange Relationship between Virtue and Violence in Human Evolution. New York: Pantheon Books.

[67] Hawks, J. (2019). The Goodness Paradox: A Review. Retrieved from https://johnhawks.net

[68] Fallon, J. (2013). The Psychopath Inside: A Neuroscientist's Personal Journey into the Dark Side of the Brain. New York: Penguin Group.

[69] National Institutes of Health (NIH). (n.d.). Testosterone. Retrieved from https://www.nih.gov

[70] The Association of Women's Healthcare, The major role of estrogen in women's health, online retrieved 11/12/2023; https://www.chicagoobgyn.com/blog/the-major-role-of-estrogen-in-womens-health

[71] Nelson, L. M. (2009). Clinical practice: Primary ovarian insufficiency. The New England Journal of Medicine, 360(6), 606-614.

[72] Zhao, L., & Ruan, L. (2016). The role of estradiol in male sexual function and spermatogenesis: Current perspectives. Andrology, 4(2), 183-191.

[73] Carre, M. T., & McCormick, C. M. (2008). Increased testosterone in human males enhances response to provocation, but not aggression per se. Psychological Science, 19(3), 225-233.

[74] Craig, S. (1992). Men, masculinity, and the media. Sage Publications.

[75] Shoemaker, D. (2013). The squared circle: Life, death, and professional wrestling. Penguin.

[76] Levy, J. (2014). The power and limits of the Overton Window. National Affairs, 20, 70–81.

[77] Farrell, W., & Gray, J. (2018). The boy crisis: Why our boys are struggling and what we can do about it. BenBella Books.

[78] Reeves, R. V. (2022). Of boys and men: Why the modern male is struggling, why it matters, and what to do about it. Brookings Institution Press

[79] Sommers, C. H. (2000/2013). The war against boys: How misguided policies are harming our young men. Simon & Schuster.

[80] Hawley, J. (2023). Manhood: The masculine virtues America needs. Regnery Publishing.

[81] Vincent, N. (2006). Self-made man: My year disguised as a man. Viking.

[82] U.S. Department of Education, National Center for Education Statistics. (2020). Digest of Education Statistics, 2019 (NCES 2020-009). https://nces.ed.gov

[83] Pew Research Center. (2023). Gender pay gap in U.S. held steady in 2022. https://www.pewresearch.org

[84] Livingston, G., & Parker, K. (2011). A tale of two fathers. Pew Research Center. https://www.pewresearch.org

[85] Case, A., & Deaton, A. (2020). Deaths of despair and the future of capitalism. Princeton University Press.

[86] Christina Hoff Sommers, The War Against Boys: How Misguided Policies Are Harming Our Young Men (New York: Simon & Schuster, 2000).

[87] Richard V. Reeves, Of Boys and Men: Why the Modern Male Is Struggling, Why It Matters, and What to Do About It (Washington, DC: Brookings Institution Press, 2022).

[88] The Boy Crisis (2018), p.28

[89] Sommers, C. H. (2000/2013). The war against boys: How misguided policies are harming our young men. Simon & Schuster.

[90] Rosenthal, R., & Jacobson, L. (1968). Pygmalion in the classroom: Teacher expectation and pupils' intellectual development. Holt, Rinehart & Winston.

91 Farrell, W., & Gray, J. (2018). The boy crisis: Why our boys are struggling and what we can do about it. BenBella Books.

92 Sommers, C. H. (2000/2013). The war against boys: How misguided policies are harming our young men. Simon & Schuster. pp.16

93 Jessica Semega, Melissa Kollar, John Creamer, and Abinash Mohanty. Report Number P60-266 Income and Poverty in the United States: 2018. Table B-1. People in Poverty by Selected Characteristics: 2017 and 2018 [<1.0 MB]

94 John Creamer, Emily A. Shrider, Kalee Burns, and Frances Chen. Poverty in the United States: 2021, September 13, 2022. Report Number P60-277 Table A-1. People in Poverty by Selected Characteristics: 2020 and 2021 [<1.0 MB]

95 U.S. Census Bureau. (2022). Income and poverty in the United States: 2021 (P60-277). U.S. Government Printing Office. https://www.census.gov

96 Quinn, P. O., & Madhoo, M. (2014). A review of attention-deficit/hyperactivity disorder in women and girls: Uncovering this hidden diagnosis. The Primary Care Companion for CNS Disorders, 16(3). https://doi.org/10.4088/PCC.13r01596; Christina Hoff Sommers, The War against Boys: How Misguided Policies Are Harming Our Young Men (New York: Simon & Schuster, 2000).

97 Barkley, R. A. (2015). Attention-deficit hyperactivity disorder: A handbook for diagnosis and treatment (4th ed.). Guilford Press.

98 Farrell, W., & Gray, J. (2018). The boy crisis: Why our boys are struggling and what we can do about it. BenBella Books.

99 Richard V. Reeves, Of Boys and Men; Christina Hoff Sommers, The War Against Boys; Warren Farrell, The Boy Crisis.

100 Gibbons, W. (2004). The tale of the boiling frog. BMJ, 329(7477), 1496. https://doi.org/10.1136/bmj.329.7477.1496

101 Ignatiev, N. (1995). How the Irish became white. Routledge; Jacobson, M. F. (1998). Whiteness of a different color: European immigrants and the alchemy of race. Harvard University Press.

102 Fischer, D. H. (1970). Historians' fallacies: Toward a logic of historical thought. Harper & Row; Hunt, L. (2002). Against presentism. Perspectives on History. American Historical Association.

103 Jackson, C. K., Johnson, R. C., & Persico, C. (2016). The effects of school spending on educational and economic outcomes: Evidence from school finance reforms. The Quarterly Journal of Economics, 131(1), 157–218. https://doi.org/10.1093/qje/qjv036

104 Farrell, W., & Gray, J. (2018). The boy crisis: Why our boys are struggling and what we can do about it. BenBella Books.

105 Crick, N. R., & Grotpeter, J. K. (1995). Relational aggression, gender, and social-psychological adjustment. Child Development, 66(3), 710–722. https://doi.org/10.2307/1131945; Olweus, D. (1993). Bullying at school: What we know and what we can do. Blackwell.

106 Hinduja, S., & Patchin, J. W. (2010). Bullying, cyberbullying, and suicide. Archives of Suicide Research, 14(3), 206–221. https://doi.org/10.1080/13811118.2010.494133; Nixon, C. L. (2014). Current perspectives: The impact of cyberbullying on adolescent health. Adolescent Health, Medicine and Therapeutics, 5, 143–158. https://doi.org/10.2147/AHMT.S36456

107 Sommers, C. H. (2000). The war against boys: How misguided feminism is harming our young men. New York, NY: Simon & Schuster.

108 Pahlke, E., Hyde, J. S., & Allison, C. M. (2014). The effects of single-sex compared with coeducational schooling on students' performance and attitudes: A meta-analysis. Psychological Bulletin, 140(4), 108, 1042–1072. https://doi.org/10.1037/a0035740

109 National Institute of Mental Health. (n.d.). Attention-Deficit/Hyperactivity Disorder. U.S. Department of Health and Human Services. https://www.nimh.nih.gov/health/topics/attention-deficit-hyperactivity-disorder-adhd

110 Digital Therapeutics Alliance. (n.d.). What is digital therapeutics? https://dtxalliance.org

111 Akili Interactive. (2020, June 15). Akili announces FDA clearance of EndeavorRx for pediatric ADHD. https://www.akiliinteractive.com; UCSF. (2020, June 15). FDA approves first video game for children with ADHD. https://www.ucsf.edu

112 Clinton, H. R. (1996). It takes a village: And other lessons children teach us. Simon & Schuster.

113 National Center for Education Statistics. (2020). Digest of Education Statistics 2019 (NCES 2020-009). U.S. Department of Education. https://nces.ed.gov/programs/digest/

114 Daniel Voyer and Susan D. Voyer, "Gender Differences in Scholastic Achievement: A Meta-Analysis," Psychological Bulletin 140, no. 4 (2014): 1174–1204, https://doi.org/10.1037/a0036620

115 Mary Steen, Why Dads and Their Babies Need to Go Skin to Skin, Scientific American, The Conversation US, 6/18/2023. Digital

116 Farrell, Warren, and John Gray. 2018. The Boy Crisis: Why Our Boys Are Struggling and What We Can Do About It. Dallas, TX: BenBella Books.

117 Ibid

118 Pond, M. (Writer), & Silverman, D. (Director). (1989, December 17). Simpsons roasting on an open fire (Season 1, Episode 1) [TV series episode]. In J. L. Brooks, M. Groening, & S. Simon (Executive producers), The Simpsons. Gracie Films; 20th Century Fox Television.

119 IACOVIELLO, Vincenzo et al. Is traditional masculinity still valued? Men's perceptions of how different reference groups value traditional masculinity norms. In: The Journal of Men's Studies, 2021. doi: 10.1177/10608265211018803

120 https://www.pewresearch.org/social-trends/2024/10/17/public-views-on-men-and-masculinity/

121 https://acf.gov/ofa/faq/national-responsible-fatherhood-clearinghouse

122 https://globalfatherhoodfoundation.org/

123 https://www.mencare.org/

124 Michael E. Lamb , Natasha J. Cabrera , Ross D. Parke , Philip Hwang , Philip A. Cowan and Carolyn Pape Cowan , Rob Palkovitz and Duncan Fisher | May 2019, https://childandfamilyblog.com/global-fatherhood-charter/

125 Michael E. Lamb , Natasha J. Cabrera , Ross D. Parke , Philip Hwang , Philip A. Cowan and Carolyn Pape Cowan , Rob Palkovitz and Duncan Fisher | May 2019 https://childandfamilyblog.com/global-fatherhood-charter/

126 https://thedadedge.com/podcast/

127 Farrell, Warren, and John Gray. 2018. The Boy Crisis: Why Our Boys Are Struggling and What We Can Do About It. Dallas, TX: BenBella Books.

128 Appendix Table 2. Comparison of Custodial Parent Population and Those With Child Support Agreements, Supposed to Receive Child Support, and Received Child Support: 1993–2017—C chrome-extension://efaidnbmnnnibpcajpcglclefindmkaj/https://www.census.gov/content/dam/Census/library/publications/2020/demo/p60-269.pdf Census.gov

129 Hyunjoon Um, The Role of Child Support Debt on the Development of Mental Health Problems among Nonresident Fathers https://ffcws.princeton.edu/sites/g/files/toruqf4356/files/wp19-05-ff.pdf

130 Farrell, Warren, and John Gray. 2018. The Boy Crisis: Why Our Boys Are Struggling and What We Can Do About It. Dallas, TX: BenBella Books.

131 Vincent, Norah. Self-Made Man: One Woman's Year Disguised as a Man. New York: Viking, 2006, 49–50.

132 Farreras, I. G. (2023). History of mental illness. In R. Biswas-Diener & E. Diener (Eds), Noba textbook series: Psychology. Champaign, IL: DEF publishers. Retrieved from http://noba.to/65w3s7ex

133 Farreras, I. G. (2023). History of mental illness. In R. Biswas-Diener & E. Diener (Eds), Noba textbook series: Psychology. Champaign, IL: DEF publishers. Retrieved from http://noba.to/65w3s7ex

134 Rössler W. The stigma of mental disorders: A millennia-long history of social exclusion and prejudices. EMBO Rep. 2016 Sep;17(9):1250-3. doi: 10.15252/embr.201643041. Epub 2016 Jul 28. PMID: 27470237; PMCID: PMC5007563.

135 Farreras, I. G. (2023). History of mental illness. In R. Biswas-Diener & E. Diener (Eds), Noba textbook series: Psychology. Champaign, IL: DEF publishers. Retrieved from http://noba.to/65w3s7ex

136 Richards, Graham. A History of Modern Psychology: The Quest for a Science of the Mind. London: Routledge, 2010.; Porter, Roy. Madness: A Brief History. Oxford: Oxford University Press, 2002.; Ellenberger, Henri F. The

Discovery of the Unconscious: The History and Evolution of Dynamic Psychiatry. New York: Basic Books, 1970.

[137] American Psychiatric Association, "DSM Frequently Asked Questions," Psychiatry.org, accessed October 26, 2025, https://www.psychiatry.org/psychiatrists/practice/dsm/frequently-asked-questions

[138] American Psychiatric Association. "DSM Frequently Asked Questions." American Psychiatric Association. https://www.psychiatry.org/psychiatrists/practice/dsm/frequently-asked-questions#:~:text=DSM%20contains%20descriptions%2C%20symptoms%20and,in%20research%20on%20mental%20disorders

[139] American Psychiatric Association. "DSM Frequently Asked Questions." American Psychiatric Association. https://www.psychiatry.org/psychiatrists/practice/dsm/frequently-asked-questions#:~:text=DSM%20contains%20descriptions%2C%20symptoms%20and,in%20research%20on%20mental%20disorders

[140] Oxford Languages. "Psychoanalysis." Oxford Languages. Accessed October 29, 2025. https://languages.oup.com/google-dictionary/en

[141] Raypole, Crystal. "Types of Therapy: Choosing the Right One for You." Healthline. Last modified August 1, 2019. https://www.healthline.com/health/types-of-therapy

[142] Reamer, David. "Community Mental Health Act of 1963." National Library of Medicine, National Institutes of Health, published October 27, 2016. https://www.ncbi.nlm.nih.gov/books/NBK553117/

[143] Bell, J. (1980). The Mental Health Systems Act of 1980. DttP: Documents to the People, 9(5), 21-22.

[144] Bell, J. (1980). The Mental Health Systems Act of 1980. DttP: Documents to the People, 9(5), 21-22.

[145] Bell, J. (1980). The Mental Health Systems Act of 1980. DttP: Documents to the People, 9(5), 21-22.

[146] "Mental Health Systems Act of 1980." National Archives and Records Administration. Accessed October 29, 2025. https://www.jimmycarterlibrary.gov/research/mhs_act

147 Bell, Katherine. "The Mental Health System Act of 1980." Documents to the People 50, no. 4 (2022). https://journals.ala.org/index.php/dttp/article/view/7933/11034.

148 Rössler W. The stigma of mental disorders: A millennia-long history of social exclusion and prejudices. EMBO Rep. 2016 Sep;17(9):1250-3. doi: 10.15252/embr.201643041. Epub 2016 Jul 28. PMID: 27470237; PMCID: PMC5007563.

149 Farrell, Warren. The Boy Crisis (p. 150). BenBella Books. Kindle Edition.

150 Gianluca Gini, PhD; Tiziana Pozzoli, PhD, Bullied Children and Psychosomatic Problems: A Meta-analysis Pediatrics (2013) 132 (4): 720–729. https://publications.aap.org/pediatrics/article-abstract/132/4/720/64862/Bullied-Children-and-Psychosomatic-Problems-A-Meta?redirectedFrom=fulltext

151 "Quotes from The Dean Martin Celebrity Roast: Sammy Davis Jr." IMDb, www.imdb.com/title/tt4129008/quotes/

152 Don Rickles, remarks during One Night Only: An All Star Comedy Tribute to Don Rickles, Spike TV, May 6, 2014.

153 E. Butelman, et al. Overdose mortality rates for opioids and stimulant drugs are substantially higher in men than in women: State-level analysis. Neuropsychopharmacology. DOI: 10.1038/s41386-023-01601-8 (2023).

154 Follman, Mark, Gavin Aronsen, and Deanna Pan. "US Mass Shootings, 1982–2023: Data From Mother Jones' Investigation." Mother Jones, December 15, 2012. Accessed November 8, 2025. https://www.motherjones.com/politics/2012/12/mass-shootings-mother-jones-full-data/

155 Victor SE, Muehlenkamp JJ, Hayes NA, Lengel GJ, Styer DM, Washburn JJ. Characterizing gender differences in nonsuicidal self-injury: Evidence from a large clinical sample of adolescents and adults. Compr Psychiatry. 2018 Apr; 82:53-60. doi: 10.1016/j.comppsych.2018.01.009. Epub 2018 Feb 4. Erratum in: Compr Psychiatry. 2018 Oct; 86:143. PMID: 29407359; PMCID: PMC5845831.

156 Clarie Jack PhD., 6 Reasons Some People Hurt the Ones They Love...and what you can do if you're on the receiving end. Psychology Today August 10,

2020. https://www.psychologytoday.com/us/blog/women-autism-spectrum-disorder/202008/6-reasons-some-people-hurt-the-ones-they-love

[157] Clarie Jack PhD., 6 Reasons Some People Hurt the Ones They Love...and what you can do if you're on the receiving end. Psychology Today August 10, 2020. https://www.psychologytoday.com/us/blog/women-autism-spectrum-disorder/202008/6-reasons-some-people-hurt-the-ones-they-love

[158] Natasha Pritchett, You Deserve unpublished poem, written at Burning Man, 2023, used with permission.

[159] Rössler W. The stigma of mental disorders: A millennia-long history of social exclusion and prejudices. EMBO Rep. 2016 Sep;17(9):1250-3. doi: 10.15252/embr.201643041. Epub 2016 Jul 28. PMID: 27470237; PMCID: PMC5007563.

[160] American Journal of Psychiatry, AJP, 175, no. 6 (June 2018): 574–574. doi:10.1176/appi.ajp.2018.1756correction1.

[161] Maya Salam, What is Toxic Masculinity", January 22nd, 2019. New York Times, Online. https://www.nytimes.com/2019/01/22/us/toxic-masculinity.html

[162] Speckhard, A. (2023, February 23). ISIS women accused of turning teen boys into human stud farm in Syria. The Daily Beast. https://www.thedailybeast.com/isis-women-accused-of-turning-teen-boys-into-human-stud-farm-in-syria/

[163] Patrick Brzeski, Japan's Johnny Kitagawa Sex Abuse Scandal: 478 Victims Come Forward, Company Rebranding Slammed as "Ridicule", The Hollywood Reporter, October 2, 2023 11:09PM

[164] Conor Friedersdorf, The Understudied Female Sexual Predator. The Atlantic, November 28, 2016

[165] Ibid

[166] Frankenbach J, Weber M, Loschelder DD, Kilger H, Friese M. Sex drive: Theoretical conceptualization and meta-analytic review of gender differences. Psychol Bull. 2022 Oct 13. doi: 10.1037/bul0000366. Epub ahead of print. PMID: 36227317.

167 Rhode Island General Assembly, Decriminalize Sex Work for Public Health, Commission Study Document, April 25, 2022, https://www.rilegislature.gov/commissions/MIC/commdocs/4-25-2022---Decriminalize%20Sex%20Work%20For%20Public%20Health--.pdf.

168 Hossain, M., Zimmerman, C., Abas, M., Light, M., & Watts, C. (2010). The relationship of trauma to mental disorders among trafficked and sexually exploited girls and women. American Journal of Public Health, 100(12), 2442–2449. https://doi.org/10.2105/AJPH.2009.173229

169 https://rangers.fireflyartscollective.org/wiki/F.L.A.M.E

170 Lee, Bruce Quote retrieved on 11/30/2023. https://www.goodreads.com/quotes/29138-be-like-water-making-its-way-through-cracks-do-not

171 Pezirkianidis C, Galanaki E, Raftopoulou G, Moraitou D, Stalikas A. Adult friendship and wellbeing: A systematic review with practical implications. Front Psychol. 2023 Jan 24;14:1059057. doi: 10.3389/fpsyg.2023.1059057. PMID: 36760434; PMCID: PMC9902704.

172 Wikipedia. "Restorative Justice." Last modified Last modified Nov 7, 2023 https://en.wikipedia.org/w/index.php?title=Restorative_justice&action=history

173 Wikipedia. "Restorative Practices." Last modified Nov 30, 2023. https://en.wikipedia.org/wiki/Restorative_practices

174 Are Black Voters Leaving Biden?" The Run-Up podcast, November 22, 2023. Apple Podcasts. https://podcasts.apple.com/us/podcast/thanksgiving-with-the-run-up-are-black-voters/id1200361736?i=1000635783760

175 Christopher Titus, The Christopher Titus Podcast, recurring theme across multiple episodes.